ADVANCED
SEX MAGIC

ADVANCED SEX MAGIC

THE HANGING MYSTERY INITIATION

MARIA DE NAGLOWSKA

Translated from the French with an
Introduction and Notes
by Donald Traxler

Inner Traditions
Rochester, Vermont • Toronto, Canada

Inner Traditions
One Park Street
Rochester, Vermont 05767
www.InnerTraditions.com

Originally published in French in 1934 under the title *Le Mystère de la pendaison* by Éditions de la Flèche

Illustrations composed by the author and executed by R. Leflers

Library of Congress Cataloging-in-Publication Data

Naglowska, Maria de, 1883–1936.
  [Mystère de la pendaison. English]
  Advanced sex magic : the hanging mystery initiation / Maria de Naglowska ; translated from the French with an introduction and notes by Donald Traxler.
      p. cm.
Originally published in French in 1934 under the title Le mystère de la pendaison by Éditions de la Flèche
  Includes bibliographical references (p.   ) and index.
  ISBN 978-1-59477-416-4 (pbk.)
  1. Sex—Miscellanea. 2. Magic. I. Traxler, Donald. II. Title.
  BF1623.S4N3513 2011
  133.4'3—dc23

                                                                2011020766

Printed and bound in Canada by Transcontinental

10 9 8 7 6 5 4 3 2 1

Text design and layout by Priscilla Baker
This book was typeset in Garamond Premier Pro with Democratica used as a display typeface

We are not going toward Unity, we are Unity

since the nonexistent beginning.

MARIA DE NAGLOWSKA

CONTENTS

INTRODUCTION

MARIA DE NAGLOWSKA, "A RIDDLE WRAPPED IN A MYSTERY"

Donald Traxler

When Winston Churchill called Russia "a riddle wrapped in a mystery inside an enigma," he could as well have been describing a daughter of Russia named Maria de Naglowska. She was a poet, a journalist, a translator, an author, an occultist, and a mystic (the latter perhaps most of all), but few know anything about her. Those who have ever heard of her probably know her as the translator of P. B. Randolph's *Magia Sexualis*[1] (which she did far more than translate).* Others, who have shown more curiosity about her, will say that she was a Satanist (not true, though it is an impression that she fostered).†

---

*[*Magia Sexualis* has survived only in Naglowska's French translation. It is composed of several works written by Randolph (notably *The Mysteries of Eulis* and *Seership*) plus material from other sources, probably including Naglowska's own ideas. Naglowska greatly improved the style and organization of Randolph's material. —*Trans.*]

†[This question has been well covered in Appendix B of *The Light of Sex*,[2] previously published in this series. —*Trans.*]

It has taken many years to get any reliable facts about her life, partly because she told different stories about herself.[3] Her most important writings, including the book on which the present book is based, were published in very small editions (now almost impossible to get) and never translated into English. Consequently, this woman whose works should occupy a significant place in the history of Western religion, is now practically unknown, especially in English.

Maria de Naglowska was born in St. Petersburg in 1883, the daughter of a prominent Czarist family.* She went to the best schools, and got the best education that a young woman of the time could get. She fell in love with a young Jewish musician, Moise Hopenko, and married him against the wishes of her family. The rift with Maria's family caused the young couple to leave Russia, going to Germany and then to Switzerland. After Maria had given birth to three children, her young husband, a Zionist, decided to leave his family and go to Palestine. This made things very difficult for Naglowska, who was forced to take various jobs as a journalist to make ends meet. While she was living in Geneva she also wrote a French grammar for Russian immigrants to Switzerland. Unfortunately, Naglowska's libertarian ideas tended to get her into trouble with governments wherever she went. She spent most of the 1920s in Rome, and at the end of that decade she moved on to Paris.

---

*[I have drawn most of the details about Naglowska's life from the short biography titled *La Sophiale*, written by her favorite student, Marc Pluquet. It is, by far, the most reliable source.[4] —*Trans.*]

While in Rome Maria de Naglowska met Julius Evola, a
pagan traditionalist who wanted to reinstate the pantheon of
ancient Rome. Evola was also an occultist, being a member of
the Group of Ur and counting among his associates some of the
followers of Giuliano Kremmerz. It is said that Naglowska and
Evola were lovers. It is known, at least, that they were associates
for a long time. She translated one of his poems into French (the
only form in which it has survived), and he translated some of
her work into Italian.

While occultists give a great deal of weight to Naglowska's
relationship with Evola, it is clear that there must have been
other influences. Some believe that she was influenced by the
Russian sect of the Khlysti, and some believe that she knew
Rasputin (whose biography she translated). Maria, though, gave
the credit for some of her unusual ideas to an old Catholic monk
whom she met in Rome. Although Maria said that he was quite
well known there, he has never been identified.[5]

Maria said that the old monk gave her a piece of cardboard,
on which was drawn a triangle, to represent the Trinity. The
first two apexes of the triangle were clearly labeled to indicate
the Father and the Son. The third, left more indistinct, was
intended to represent the Holy Spirit. To Maria, the Holy Spirit
was feminine. We don't know how much was the monk's
teaching and how much was hers, but Maria taught that the
Father represented Judaism and reason, while the Son represented
Christianity, the heart, and an era whose end was approaching.
To Maria, the feminine Spirit represented a new era, sex, and

the reconciliation of the light and dark forces in nature.

It is mostly this idea of the reconciliation of the light and dark forces that has gotten Maria into trouble, and caused her to be thought of as a Satanist. Maria herself is partly responsible for this, having referred to herself as a "satanic woman" and used the name also in other ways in her writings. Evola, in his book *The Metaphysics of Sex,* mentioned her "deliberate intention to scandalize the reader."[6] Here is what Naglowska herself had to say about it:

Nous défendons à nos disciples de s'imaginer Satan (= l'esprit du mal ou l'esprit de la destruction) comme vivant en dehors de nous, car une telle imagination est le propre des idolâtres; mais nous reconnaissons que ce nom est vrai.

We forbid our disciples to imagine Satan (= the spirit of evil or the spirit of destruction) as living outside of us, for such imagining is proper to idolaters; but we recognize that this name is true.

In 1929, Naglowska moved to Paris, where she got the unwelcome news that she would not be given a work permit. Deprived of the ability to be employed in a regular job, she would have to depend on her own very considerable survival skills. She began work on the book for which she is best known today, her "translation" of *Magia Sexualis,*[7] by Paschal Beverly Randolph. This work by the American hermetic and sex theorist is known only in Naglowska's "translation." I have put the word "translation" in quotation marks because it is really a compilation. Only about two-thirds of the work can be identified as being from Randolph. The rest is from sources only beginning to be identified, or from Naglowska herself, and the organization of the material is clearly her contribution as well.

While Naglowska was working on *Magia Sexualis,* she began giving lectures or "conferences" on an original teaching of her own. She called it the Doctrine of the Third Term of the Trinity. Her "conferences" were at first often held in cafés. The proprietors of these venues were pleased with the influx of patrons and often gave Maria free food and coffee. In a short time her following grew to the point where she could afford to rent a large, bare room, which held thirty to forty people* for her private meetings.[8] It was thus that Maria survived.

Maria's income was supplemented by her publishing endeavors. After the 1931 publication of *Magia Sexualis,* Naglowska turned to writing original works. One of these, *Le Rite sacré de l'amour magique,* a metaphysical novelette apparently containing

---

*[According to Pluquet in *La Sophiale,* there were only 30–40 people in the hall when it was full, and the overflow stood in a *baie vitrée,* or glassed-in bay, which separated the hall from the entrance. The hall in question was the old Studio Raspail at 46 Rue Vavin (not to be confused with the present cinema on Bd. Raspail). The building now houses an Italian restaurant that has a capacity of 120 seats. The space may have been enlarged, or it may not. The low divider that formed the baie vitrée is still there, but it no longer seems to have glass over it. It would take a sizable crowd to fill the space and still have overflow standing in the entryway. On page 14, Pluquet states that all of these "conferences" were taken down in shorthand by a certain Mr. Dufour. Unfortunately, these shorthand notes have not yet surfaced. —*Trans.*]

elements of her own life, was published as a supplement to her street newspaper in early 1932, having earlier been serialized there.[9] The little newspaper, to which she and other occultists contributed, was called *La Flèche, Organe d'Action Magique.* It was the public voice of her magical group, *La Confrérie de la Flèche d'Or.*

Later in 1932, Naglowska published *La Lumière du Sexe,* published in English in the current series as *The Light of Sex.*[10] In 1934, she published *Le Mystère de la Pendaison,* or *The Hanging Mystery,** on which the current book is based. These two books were required reading for even First Degree initiation into Naglowska's magical group,[11] and contained all of the doctrine of her new religion, the Third Term of the Trinity, and much of its ritual. They are thus of paramount importance for understanding Maria de Naglowska and her teaching. They are also, unfortunately, quite rare, having been originally published in small editions of about five hundred copies. To my knowledge, the translations in the present series are the first that have been made of any of Naglowska's original works into English.

Naglowska is said to have been very psychic. She predicted the catastrophe of the Second World War,[12] and in 1935 she foresaw her own death.[13] Knowing that she was going to die, she refused to reprint *The Light of Sex* and *The Hanging Mystery,* which had

---

*[The title of this edition is *Advanced Sex Magic: The Hanging Mystery Initiation.* In remaining true to the translation from French, we will refer to it as *The Hanging Mystery* throughout this text. —*Ed.*]

both sold out. She told her followers that nothing would be able to be done to spread her teachings for two or three generations. She went to live with her daughter in Zurich, and it was there that she died, at the age of fifty-two, on April 17, 1936.

Maria was influential among the Surrealists, and they seem to have influenced her own writing. Naglowska's sessions are said to have been attended by the avant-garde and the notorious of the time, including Man Ray, William Seabrook, Michel Leiris, Georges Bataille, and André Breton. Jean Paulhan, for whom *L'Histoire d'O* was written, is also said to have attended. I have not yet been able to trace these often-made claims to reliable, original sources, so for the present they should be regarded as hearsay. We know, however, that surrealist poet and painter Camille Bryen was a member of Naglowska's group,[14] as the writer Ernest Gengenbach appears to have been, and it seems significant that one of the best studies of Naglowska was done by another surrealist, Sarane Alexandrian.[15] Maria's French was impeccable and her style clean and powerful, but she used words in a symbolic, highly idiosyncratic way. Shortly before she left Paris, she told her disciples that her teachings "would need to be translated into clear and accessible language for awakened women and men who would not necessarily be symbolists."[16] Taking this as my directive, I have added extensive explanatory footnotes to the texts of *The Light of Sex* and this *Advanced Sex Magic*.

Due to the small editions and her refusal to reprint them, plus her early death and the unfortunate arrival of World War

II, Maria's influence seems hardly to have extended beyond Montparnasse. This needs to change. With the perspective granted by time, we can now see that Naglowska was an important mystic of the twentieth century. At the very least she deserves a place in the history of religion for having achieved within the Western tradition the full, non-dualistic realization typified by the major Upanishads. In so doing, she has bequeathed to us a vision that, while idiosyncratic, is also powerful and uplifting.

DONALD TRAXLER began working as a professional translator (Benemann Translation Service, Berlitz Translation Service) in 1963. Later, he did translations for several institutions in the financial sector. On his own time he translated poetry and did his first metaphysical translations in the early 1980s. He later combined these interests, embarking on an ambitious, multi-year project to translate the works of Lalla (also known as Lalleshvari, or Lal Ded), a beloved fourteenth-century poet of Kashmir Shaivism. That project is still not complete, but many of the translations have become favorites of contemporary leaders of the sect. He is currently focusing on Western mysticism, and is halfway through a four-book series on Maria de Naglowska for Inner Traditions. He is contemplating a major project on another European mystic and an eventual return to and completion of the Lalla project. Except for Lalla, he translates from Spanish, French, and Italian. All of his projects are labors of love.

ADVANCED
SEX
MAGIC

Dedicated to the Sovereign Pontiff Pius XI,
the Pope of the Critical Hour

preface

THE INITIATIC
RITE OF THE THIRD
DEGREE

The book that we are offering to our friends and readers today completes the volume that appeared in 1932 under the title *The Light of Sex*.

There we give the description of the great initiatic rite of the third degree, called the Hanging Test, and some doctrinal details, definitively situating the religion of the Third Term of the Trinity, which we preach, in confrontation with Christianity, on the one hand, and with Judaism, on the other.

We do not occupy ourselves especially with modern spiritual movements, such as Theosophy or Spiritualism, because as we have said elsewhere, we do not see in the currents of ideas coming from India or the Orient in general the constructive elements that could serve as a base for the new rebuilding of Europe's theological, social, and moral edifice.

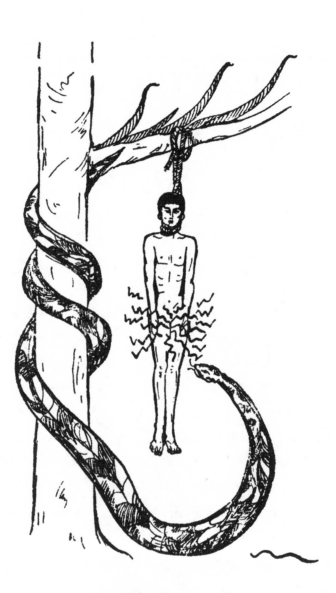

The Hanged Man

As we have said since the beginning of our activity in Paris in 1930, the European peoples are essentially destined to continue the Triangle, of which the first two branches have been and still are Judaism and Christianity, which have prepared what we will do now in the light of the religion of the Third Term.

In human terms, the principal characteristic of our Triangle lies in the understanding, whether conscious or instinctive, of the solidarity that spiritually joins all members of the same church together into a single indivisible bloc, while honoring the idea, nonexistent in the oriental systems, of the saving value for the others of the merit of the best.

Currently, this great Western idea seems to have been pushed into the background following the infiltration of individualism among us, having come from the Orient via certain philosophers of the decadent era, but, not having perverted other than the intellectual strata of our peoples, this same individualism is already crumbling before the push of politico-philosophical activism, determined, also, precisely by the incompatibility between Eastern individualism and the profound collectivist conscience of the West, reinforced in the peoples of Europe above all by the fertile action of Apostolic Roman Catholicism.

One will find our definitive statements in this regard in *The Hanging Mystery.*

Divinely, the mission of our Triangle consists in redirecting the Spirit of Evil onto the good path, or, in other words, the Redemption of Satan.

It is because this is true that it is time to recognize that, while the East applies itself to conquering Evil by its destruction, the true goal of the Christianity of Europe has been from the beginning exactly the opposite: the victory of Evil itself by means of its transformation into Good.

And, in affirming this, we maintain that even the era of apparent decay, which we are passing through at this time, is on track in the sense that the chaotic overflowing of all passions that we are witnessing at this moment is nothing else than the first clumsy steps of evil reformed.

We regret that our opponents hesitate to enter into closely argued discussion with us about these problems. Light could very certainly be cast on many shadowy points in a frank and honest oratorical combat.

We would like to hope that the apparition of this book would at last set off the debates for which we have wished.

Maria de Naglowska

THE HUMAN TREE

The Brotherhood of the Knights of the Golden Arrow, whose doctrine we have presented in our preceding volume, entitled *The Light of Sex,* is still in the shadows, because the hour of its triumph has not yet sounded.

But, soon, the veil of red clouds that envelops the City of the Future will be dissipated, and then the West first, and afterward the East, will recognize the marvelous work accomplished by the Magnificent Invisible Heroes who lead humanity, without the latter's awareness, toward the third phase of our Triangle, the phase of the Third Term of the Trinity, whose coming is near and whose light will be splendid.

On the threshold of the New Day, at this supreme moment, which still separates us from happiness, and which is the most painful because a mother suffers when the head of her child appears, it is useful to finally know what Man has done on this earth for the last nearly two thousand years, and to understand the reasons and the principal cause of his apparent decay.

We say "Man" and not "men" on purpose, because he who evolves through the many races and the successive Triangles of human history is a Single One.

The shadows of our century, the lies spread because of our petty disputes and our sterile vanities, have obscured this primordial truth in the personal consciences of the mortal genus of the Unique Man, causing the humans that one meets on the agitated streets of our towns to imagine that they are individual entities whose egoism would be justified.

No man carries within himself the root of his life. Just as the foliage of a tree, we all depend on a single root that is common to all of us, and from which no one can make himself independent without dying irremediably and without causing a more or less considerable hurt to the human plant as a whole.

Our common root, the root of all humanity, is lost in the depths of our earth, and no one knows from what fire it nourishes itself, because each imagines that the air that he breathes and the sap that he digests are his and for him alone.

No one knows, today, that no heart beats and no nerve contracts for the life of just one, and all are unaware, alas, that the act of each one is an act of all, accomplished by one but coming from all and impacting all.

The ignorance of this fundamental and ineluctable law of the presence of each in all and of all in each would not be a bad thing for humanity as a whole and it would not throw us into decline and later into the degradation of the lower animal kingdom, if the branches that support the leaves of the human tree and bind them to the unique trunk were not damaged and soon dried up.

The individuals making up the foliage—the human masses—could well have lived in their ignorance and in the illusion of their egoistic particularism without harming the whole of humanity, if the spiritual hierarchies, whose role is precisely to bind them without their knowledge to the main branches, thus assuring the health of the whole tree, had not been dried up, that is to say deprived little by little of the Life-giving Spirit, by the methodical replacement, in the hierarchic grades, of worthy men by unworthy ones, by madmen, and if—to speak the incorrect language of the crowds—the leaders of the masses had remained men of the elite and had not become simpletons, as silly as the very ones they pretended to direct.

For, if the blind are led by a man with good eyes, all can arrive at a safe haven, but if the leader is himself blind, and is not able to spot the bridge that leads to the other side—the side of the New Era—they all remain at the river's edge and go nowhere.

Now, not to advance, not to increase, is to die. The north wind arrives soon, it rips the malnourished leaves from the tree, and the decomposition of the latter is then rapid, because from the depths of the earth the root can no longer send them the strength and the blood necessary for growth.

Life is then extinguished in the people, and the bad hierarchies perish first.

This is what is happening now among our humanity; suffering because of the second birthing of our Triangle . . . More than nineteen centuries separate us from the first . . .

Two branches, two new shoots, had formed on the tree of human life, when the great Crucified One expired on the wood of the Redemption, projecting into the world the will of the No, having become white in the mystery of the Passion and whose effect would have been disastrous if, at the same minute and in the shadow of the cross, the traitor necessary to the divine work had not meted out justice to himself, putting the cord around his neck and contorting thus in the root the Spirit purified by the Christ.

For—and this is a revelation of cardinal importance—if Judas Iscariot had not first betrayed his Master and then experienced the fiercest remorse, crowned by the voluntary punishment of the Hanging, the humanity, which, in Christ and through Christ, had realized the redemption of Satan, would have been taken up with Jesus toward the origin (which never was), leaving the part of the foliage that was too green or too yellow—the new races and the old races—to the power of the forces of decaying putrefaction.

These leaves—these innumerable individuals—would have been cast into the depths of the inferior regions, from which one does not return or, at the very least, very slowly and through incalculable Triangles, in which the passage from the First Term to the Second Term, and from this to the Third Term is incessantly repeated.

It would have been, in effect, the end of the world and the last judgment, desired by the Christ.

But thanks to the crime of Judas, followed by his remorse and initiatic hanging, the people in whom and by whom the humanity of our Triangle had lit their torch of Reason,* which binds the destiny of Satan† to that of Man, the people of Israel remained outside of the Redemption worked by the Christ.

By this fact he reestablished in the tree of human life resistance to the carrying off of the leaves toward the origin, that is to say toward nothingness, and consequently assured the permanence on our earth for the whole period of the Second Term—the period of the Cross—of the struggle between the Yes and the No, which maintains Life, that is to say God, in visible manifestation, willed since the beginning (which never was) by He who is, who was, and who will be, the Unique and Incomparable Living Being of whom no man will ever know the Name save at the supreme moment of initiatic suffocation by means of hanging . . . and how many are they, those who face this fearsome test?

The work of the Christ, on the one hand, and the work of Judas, on the other, caused two new shoots to be born on the

---

*[As explained in the first book, *The Light of Sex*, Naglowska's system, the Third Term of the Trinity, equated Judaism with Reason, Christianity with the Heart, and the New Era of the Third Term with Sex. —*Trans.*]

†[In Naglowska's strange, symbolic language, "Satan" represents, among other things, human reason, as opposed to what she called "direct knowledge." Naglowska considered the former, reason, to be more characteristic of men, and the latter to be more characteristic of women. —*Trans.*]

tree of human life, between which soon formed the third: the young branch composed of the peoples and races who awaited in the North their turn to descend into the arena of the great life-or-death struggles, by which the forward march of God himself is realized. God is Life.*

The branch born from the work of Judas, the black branch, massed in itself all of the positive vigor of Satan attached to human Reason, and, resolutely departing from the vertical line of the Fall, along which God (= Life) had fought against the revolt of Man, making the sword of his Word increasingly sharp, it (the black branch) oriented the people of Israel toward the sorrow and suffering of the cruel exile . . .

We know that the Freedman leaves on a voyage after having received the terrifying baptism of fire of Reason. He wanders, then, over the earth and nowhere does he find rest. Much later he comes back to the Temple of Love, where his Fiancée awaits him. He presents himself for the test of the third degree, and if he triumphs in accordance with the "testimonies" that we will read later on, he is admitted to the number of the Venerable Warriors, who have understanding and know what is just . . .

The Romans, who in the distant era of the first Night of our Triangle were the unknowing instrument of the Magnificent Invisible Heroes, whose glory will soon be manifested, resisted the penetration of the dissolving influence of nascent Christianity

---

*["God is Life" is the supreme tenet of Naglowska's new religion. It's corollary, "Life is God," is also true. —*Trans.*]

into the Italian peninsula for quite a long time, the influence of this white branch in which the formidable will of Jesus to do away with the visible world in order to redirect humanity toward the Origin—Chaos or nothingness—was already weakening as he took up a body.

Instead they received the black shoot, while prudently creating the Diaspora of the House of Israel.

This inoculated them against the contorted strength of the No and thus prepared them for the later digestion of the already weakened White, so that later when Rome proclaimed its "Catholic, Apostolic, and Roman" Christianity, the will to annihilate the world to get back to the origin was no longer, in the latter, more than a patient hope of gaining "heaven" and the "afterlife" by means of personal merit, that is to say, by the individual effort of each one.

The free will of each man—of the leaf attached to the branch—was a severe dogma, imposed upon the faithful in order to bar their way toward the Redemption worked by Christ and for participation in which faith alone was necessary. Charity makes faith lukewarm.

Roman Catholicism was a solid Church. The White took on there, little by little, all the colors of the rainbow, while the great and bitter struggle between the contorted Yes and No* was

---

*[This is best explained in the first book, *The Light of Sex*. There it is said that the Yes represents the Will to Live, while the No represents the Will to Die. The Yes is stronger, which is why we are here to discuss it. On the other hand, the interaction of both is necessary to the continued existence of Life. —*Trans.*]

pursued outside of the human crowd, which only rarely heard the furious cries of the opposing winds and never knew the causes.

The task undertaken by Roman Catholicism was truly grandiose: to protect Humanity—the new branch of the young races and the aged foliage of the whole tree—from the equally dangerous influences of the White and the Black,* born respectively from the Cross and from the Cord and determined, the one, to draw the souls—the blood formed in the leaves—into a blessed rapture toward the Heaven of the Father, where all would have formed a single transparent Cone, glorious and immobile, and the other, to cast into the earth the mad will to conquer the law of life engendering death, which Humanity knew for a second in Judas and through Judas. The triumph of the Hanged Man!

The Roman Catholic Church was wished by those who preside over human destinies and orient their historic course. That is why it was strong and lasted a long time.

But, when the green shoot that it protected—the branch composed of the new races grafted onto the old Roman trunk— became solid and brown wood, the Magnificent Invisible Heroes distanced themselves from the Church, which they had protected, and created a current hostile to it in the north of Europe, spreading around and soon within the Church itself a quiet corruption.

This current rapidly became a very wide river, and it divided

---

*[These symbolic terms do not represent races. They represent the Positive and the Negative, the Yes and the No. Since both must always be present, though in varying proportions, they could also be thought of as the Yang and the Yin of Taoism. They are equally dangerous because without both life could not exist. —*Trans.*]

itself into many streams, to be able to work everywhere in an effective manner.

The water of this river contains various and powerful poisons, whose action is still necessary in this deep Night, where the second Birthing of our Triangle is accomplished, but Man renewed will soon be born, and then the poisons will be withdrawn from the water that bathes them.

One will understand then that the struggles and the sufferings that characterized the twenty centuries of the Christian Era—the painful Era of the Cross and the Cord—were beautiful and necessary.

Only the waste, and above all the hierarchies, damaged by the corruption caused by the poisons spread to that effect, will perish in the depths of the earth, but the wholesome and holy elements of all humanity will recognize the New Sun and will with a common accord rebuild the Temple of the Third Era, the Temple of the Arrow, whence humanity, regenerated by the Golden Mass, will be launched very high and very far. After the celebration of this Mass it will no longer be possible to believe in the essential separation between and among individuals.

All in each, each in all, such will be the new Chant.

And then there will no longer be unrecognized worth, because jealousy will be dead.

The Brotherhood of the Knights of the Golden Arrow will come out of the shadows that have enveloped it and will openly direct the work of the new reorganization.

The pages that follow prepare the way for these events.

JESUS OF NAZARETH

The doctrine of the Third Term of the Trinity, which is the dogmatic base upon which humanity will soon build its New Edifice, after the definitive collapse of the Temple of the Second Era, this doctrine, whose principal teachings and preparatory ritual we have revealed in *The Light of Sex,* recognizes in Jesus the Blessed Man, who has been able to climb the dangerous slope of satanic* initiation up to the supreme summit, on whose height the disciple fully and definitively incarnates the formidable adversary of God (= Life) who says No to the visible manifestation of the divine powers, that is to say to the Universe.

---

*[Naglowska did not believe in Satan as an entity outside of ourselves, but rather as the will to destruction that must be reformed and turned to good, the will to die that must become the will to live. It is a complex symbolism, best explained in *The Light of Sex.* At times "Satan" also represents becoming enmeshed in human reasoning with its limitations (as opposed to direct and intuitive perception, which she referred to as direct intelligence). Naglowska considered the enmeshment in human reason with its limitations to be characteristic of the brains of males, and "direct intelligence" to be characteristic of the brains of females. —*Trans.*]

Recognizing this, the New Doctrine affirms the true sanctity of the act of the great Moses who, in the Arabian desert, seeing the misery and weakness of the people who had emerged victorious from the poisoned waters of the Red Sea, hung a serpent on a cross* and cried out, "Look upon this with faith, and you will be saved."

The weak man, the child-man, takes *"salut"* (safety, salvation, welfare) to mean his own well-being, that is why he accepts the manna that is given to him.

But the aware man, the adult man, knows that well-being does not exist, if it is not for all. He refuses the manna, and goes on suffering.

Jesus of Nazareth suffered to the end, because he wished the well-being of all.

Well-being? . . . Dissolution in the blessedness of the indecipherable, of the whole Human Tree, for Jesus knew that this Tree was within himself, as he himself was within the Tree.

The people—the leaves attached to the branch—didn't understand him and didn't like him, except insofar as he alleviated their misery. But the chiefs of the House of Israel who knew the Work that he wished to accomplish, hated him, judging him to be dangerous.

Ultimately, the will of the Christ was able to triumph,

---

*This is apparently a reference to Numbers 21:8–9, in which Moses makes an image of a serpent and hangs it on a "standard" (Hebrew *nes*). This "standard" has become a "cross" in Naglowska's mind.

because what he proposed was not difficult. It sufficed for humans, and in particular for the sons of Israel, those near to him, to attach themselves to Jesus of Nazareth with all their heart, with all their soul and with all their thought, to abandon all preoccupation concerning the earthly world, to let grow in themselves the faith that the Master had breathed into every person who did not resist too much, to let themselves be drawn, absorbed, into his prodigious will, wholly bent toward the Heaven of the Father, where there is no longer anything but an immense joyful song, the song of the unarticulated Word.

If all humans had loved the Christ with all their heart, with all their soul, and with all their thought, the world would have ended, and Satan, happy in his triumph, would have said "My Father" to God (= Life).

It would have been the final catastrophe, because God himself would have perished in the filial embrace of Satan reformed.

Now, God cannot die, for in his essence He is Life, Life that manifests itself, grows, and changes.

The visible world exists because of that.

And also because of that, not being able to admit the Redemption as Jesus wished it, the Father pushed his Son away, who gave up his last breath on the cross, crying out: "My God, My God, why hast thou forsaken me?"

In the absolute night that enveloped him then, no word made itself heard in response to his unprecedented cry of desolation, but in the Temple of the First Era—the era of the Fall and of the Torch of Reason—the veil that separated the Mystery from the multitude of the circumcised was torn from top to bottom, and the sacred Ark, which contained the Rod symbolizing procreation, appeared to the eyes of all. The Universe would continue to exist!

The doctrine of the Third Term of the Trinity requires of its disciples a profound veneration for the memory of the Christ, the King of the Jews, Jesus of Nazareth.

In him and through him, all humanity achieved, at the beginning of the Second Era, absolute Whiteness, the perfect purity of Satan,* reflected upon the human collectivity after the death of Jesus, in the form of a powerful will to conquer the Fall.

Now the Fall is the very principle of procreation, of the infinite succession of generations throughout the Continuance,† which never ends.

The Fall is the precipitation of God (= Life) into Hell, where Satan protests.‡

The great Moses had elevated satanic protestation, which in the animal regions determines the brutality of the beast, to

---

*[Not as an independent entity, but as the dark and destructive force now regenerated or reformed. —*Trans.*]

†[This term, part of Naglowska's complex symbolism, was touched upon in *The Light of Sex.* It appears to represent the "contradictory harmony" of the Yes and the No (the Will to Live and the Will to Die), which makes possible the continued existence of the manifest Universe. —*Trans.*]

‡[Here, Satan = Reason, which protests endlessly against God (= Life). —*Trans.*]

the level of human reason, where satanism is nothing more than Doubt:*

"Thou shalt not know the name of God, thy Creator.

"Thou shalt not find his image either in the heavens or on the earth, or in the waters under the earth.

"Thou shalt remain inactive on the day of the Sabbath, because on this day God rested and his creation, which emanated from Doubt and from Doubt's protestation and did not know how to be other than malefic, as a duel with a dead man.

"Thou shalt remember that God, thy Creator, wishes that you should respect your father and your mother, the man and the woman who gave you life.

"Thou shalt not kill any living creature, except those that you must eat to feed yourself, or exterminate to defend yourself.

"And thou shalt respect the goods of thy neighbor, his women, his domestic animals, and the objects that belong to him, because he has acquired them at the cost of his gold or his labor, according to the Law, which subjects all to penalties.

"It is thus that thou shalt be a son of Israel, a son of the man who, in his dream, fought against God, but who, upon awakening, confessed his powerlessness, recognizing himself as the slave of God."

In Jesus and through Jesus, humanity denied its slavery. It

---

*[This is an extremely interesting definition of satanism. It helps to explain why, in one of her essays,[1] Naglowska said that all philosophers, rabbis, and Christian theologians practiced satanism. —*Trans.*]

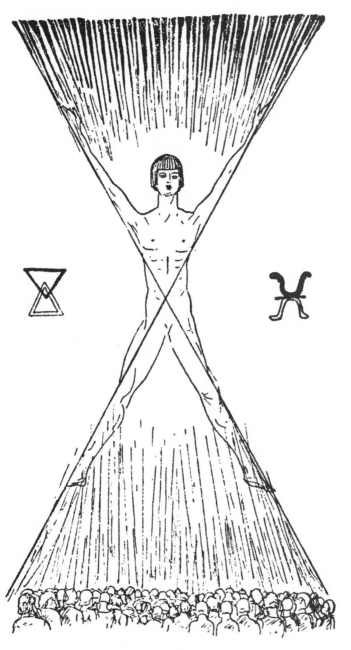

The White Cone

did it with all its heart, and with all its soul, concentrated on this sublime minute in the heart of the Redeemer, and it thus opposed the horizontal line of Negation to the vertical line of the Fall:

"Man and woman will detest their flesh, for it is an impediment to the realization of the Kingdom of Heaven.

"They will abandon their father and mother, and will not love their neighbor except in the name of Christ.

"They will know that God—the Inexpressible!—is called the Father and that he wants all of them in his impalpable region, as unreal, transparent, and sublime as Himself.

"They will not have any personal property, because every attachment to the goods of this 'lower' world weighs them down on the amorous rush toward the Beyond and the Christ.

"And they will always remember that no one can be saved except by the complete dissolution of their will and of their personal intelligence in the white Cone formed by Jesus."

The doctrine of the Third Term of the Trinity, even as it rejects this teaching of the dissolving White, requires of its disciples a deep and sincere veneration for the Crucified One, who broke the line of the Fall, while leading Life (= God) on a new path.

THE WOMAN OF
THE UNKNOWN

I n the chapels of the Brotherhood of the Knights of the Golden Arrow, where initiation is given to the young women destined to fill the role of priestesses, the following prayer is customary:

> *O Jesus, child of Nazareth, son of Mary and*
> *son of the Unknown,*
> *How many times, since my most tender*
> *youth, have I begged you to absorb me*
> *into Yourself!*
> *I still remember the great cathedrals, where*
> *I found it so sweet to hear only You,*
> *as prayer, chanted before the altar,*
> *bent a weary and wan people over the*
> *flagstones.*
> *Multiple hot tapers burned before your holy*

*image with a mystic fire, like unto my
love.*

*Oh! I see them still, those stems of pale ocher
and their golden petals, trembling in the
slightest breeze!*

*Would that I could have run down upon the
tray like a drop of wax, blessed by Your
gaze!*

*Yes, I assure you, I had understood the
Dawning of this death so sweet on the
breast of the Redeemer, and, falling
upon the rigid metal, I would have
chanted still: "Hail, my only Lord!"*

*But You remained mute in the shadows of
the church; it was in vain, each time
that I offered my soul, while the prayer
burned before the image, bending
weighed-down people over the flagstones.*

*Yes, certainly, wiser than Your faithful, and
bound, perhaps, by a secret oath, You
rejected my pure offering then because
another order was to come.*

*I don't know, Jesus of Nazareth, son of Mary
and son of the Unknown, if You, like
me, keep the memory of what was then
my childhood dream; but I tell you, I*

*who adore You still in your Contrary
and in the Dawning Day, in the furious
water of sea under storm, and in the
lightning that streaks the covered sky:*
*It is surely because of the evening fast that
was imposed then on the daughters of
the Church, that we shall soon see the
great cathedrals transform themselves
suddenly into new domes.*

*There will then be no more, in the mystic
music, of the somber allusions that bend
the crowds to the ground, and the golden
petals, trembling above the tapers, will
be a sign of love, joyous for all.*

*We shall deliver ourselves then to the
new Mass* not, as before, veiled like
penitents, but as beautiful flowers of
a splendid garland, each leaf of which
breathes the sun.*

*Before the Altar, where the new priestesses
will serenely celebrate the new rites of
love, we shall tell you then, Jesus of
Nazareth, why Mary, Your Mother, was
the woman of the Unknown.*

---

*[The "Golden Mass" —*Trans.*]

JUDAS ISCARIOT

One cannot be an adept of the religion of the Third Term of the Trinity if one does not accept the dogma that places the work of Judas alongside that of Jesus, recognizing it to be complementary to the latter in the same manner as the effort of the left leg is complementary to the effort of the right leg in the formation of a forward step.

The New Doctrine says the following in this regard:

If Jesus of Nazareth hadn't been betrayed by Judas Iscariot, his disciple and friend, the Christ would not have been martyred unless by his enemies, who would not have been able to experience remorse for it, and in this case humanity, which in Jesus and through Jesus achieved Absolute Whiteness on the cross—the leap toward the unreal heaven of the Father—would not have had the strength to form the baseline angle of the Triangle, which kept Life (= God) on earth, tracing its new path, the way of the Second Era, which is completed today.

What is remorse?

It is the second bite of the symbolic Serpent, which pierces the flesh after having pierced the soul of the initiate.

The first bite—also called the first kiss—determines the disciple's will to oppose himself to the "good," which keeps him within the moral routine, on which rests the social edifice of the preceding order.

The first kiss, or the first bite of the symbolic Serpent is, consequently, essentially revolutionary, and if it is not followed by the second, the state of soul that it causes in the one bitten remains purely destructive.

Nothing can be built in a sensible and durable fashion by the initiates who have been bitten only once by the Serpent, which in the Great School symbolizes in a general way the Adversary of God (= Life) and, in a particular way, the negation of the act of procreation, wished by Life (= God) so that the Universe may continue to exist.

At the same time, the incomplete initiates are necessary to certain periods of human or cosmic history, and this explains why the understanding of the second key sometimes disappears in the initiatic temples, rendering impossible the accomplishment of the redoubtable Hanging Mystery, which realigns the Way of God and gives expression to God's new destiny.

In the nocturnal times of the great historical cycles, such as that in which Jesus was born, this understanding is, on the contrary, present, and then those who must understand, in order to accomplish what has been written, understand and act.

In them, all humanity understands and acts, even if the

isolated individuals do not trouble themselves about it.

Jesus knew that his Passion would not have been efficacious for what was to come later if one of his friends did not betray him.

That is why, when he took his last meal with the twelve, he said to them: "I say to you, I say to you, one of you will betray me."

And while the apostles, deeply troubled, asked themselves, "Which one of us is chosen for that?" Jesus dipped a piece of bread into his wine, and offering it to Judas Iscariot, he commanded him: "What you have to do, do it quickly."

It is written in certain gospel texts: "Then Satan entered into Judas, and the latter left the room immediately to accomplish his work of betrayal."*

The bread dipped in the wine by the very hand of Jesus was, on the tongue of Judas, the Communion with the Saint, may he be blessed, who opposes himself day and night to the visible manifestation of the divine Powers, keeping the One in the Universe who is, who was, and who always will be. (See *The Light of Sex.*)

The bite having been violent, the crime of destruction that followed it had to be a capital one.

Judas went to sell his Master to the Sanhedrin.

"I will give him a fraternal kiss," he said, "and the Roman

---

*[The first part is similar to Luke 22:3; the last part must be a conflation from another text. —*Trans.*]

soldiers will recognize him by this sign. Since he calls himself the king of the Jews, the king of the people of Procreation, he must die on the cross, which symbolizes perpetuity."

And, in effect, in the garden of the olive trees, where, before the Cup, which was traced then on the nocturnal backdrop filled with shadows and with uncertain gleams, as a last invitation to choose another path, Jesus had just pronounced his definitive prayer, by which he reunited in his heart the will and the life of all those who were his—"Not all, my Father, but those whom Thou hast given me, so that they may be in Us, as I am in Thee, and as Thou art in me"—in the garden of the olive trees, where the faith of the apostles had been dulled because nothing personal remained in them at that moment, Judas, followed by the Roman soldiers, approached Jesus and, after saying to him in an ironic tone, "Greetings, my Lord," gave him a truly fraternal kiss on the cheek.

For, only a brother is the equal of his brother, in love as in hate. And do not speak to us of fraternal charity. This latter does not exist, because the gift of the brother is respect, in love and in hate.

Since Jesus wanted to vanquish the Fall of the Invisible into the Visible, to vanquish the death of Pure Spirit, Judas, his equal at that minute, offered him the chance, fraternally.

But the Calvary that the Christ climbed from that minute on, carrying upon his shoulders the symbol of eternity, the Cross upon which He was going to blossom, like a triumphant flame that devours all perishable material, transforming it into thin and volatile vapor, this Calvary, at the foot of which Judas was the equal of the Christ, reestablished an enormous distance between the two men, and, when Jesus was plunged into total night, after having let out his terrible cry of an abandoned Only Son, Judas, who heard the cry and understood all of its meaning, received the second initiatic bite and was immediately plunged into remorse.

Remorse is not regret, and it doesn't resemble the state of soul of the penitent, who wants pardon to erase his crime.

Remorse is a fire, which burns in the interior of the flesh, immobilizing thought and smothering all feelings.

True remorse is the supreme voluptuousness that comes from terror.

It is initiatic because reason, compressed by the atrocious spasm, precipitates the most formidable negation into the root of the flesh, there where Man drinks at the very source of Life (= God) the sap that binds him to the whole world, to humanity and to all the inferior and superior regions, provoking in the very place of the flesh the most violent reaction.

He who experiences that hates life, for its call is unbearable to him, and he tries to suppress it.

Judas, thus maddened, seized a rope and hanged himself.

All humanity that did not belong to Christ at that moment, and particularly the people of Israel, who had taken upon themselves the responsibility for the execution of Jesus, in crying out "his blood will be upon us and upon our children," had its part in the hanging of Judas, and when, strangling in the slipping noose, the flesh of Judas took it's last revenge, being liberated from the reasoning conscience and from the memory attached to the latter, all humanity, concentrated in him, reaffirmed, by him and in him, its will to live, keeping God within the creation.

In this way, the Pure White will find the Black in front of it, plunged again into the red blood of Man.

In vulgar language this can be translated thus: while Jesus Christ was redeeming Satan by his triumphant Passion, restoring in him all the immaculate transparency of white gold, Judas spilled it again in human flesh, in the very place where God (= Life) affirms and maintains the principle of generation and the continuity of species.

With regard to the vertical line of the Fall—the line of the precipitation of the Invisible into the Visible, to affirm the latter, while chasing Satan* (the Judaism of the First Term) away from it—the Work of Jesus and the Work of Judas are equally revolutionary. But, while the work of Jesus alone, without the complement of that of Judas, could not have any other effect than the annihilation of the Universe, the canceling out of the manifested divine powers, and the rejection of the eternal duel

---

*[Naglowska often represented the Judaism of the First Term as characterized by the principles of procreation and reason, while the Christianity of the Second Term was characterized by balance and the heart. The new religion of the Third Term (which she did not otherwise name) would be characterized by a re-spiritualization of mankind through sex and love and the agency of the (feminine) Holy/Wholesome Spirit. "Satan" here represents Reason/Doubt, which she considered characteristic of men and male-dominated societies, as opposed to the "direct intelligence," or "direct understanding" that she considered characteristic of women. —*Trans.*]

between the Yes and the No in the glacial regions where nothing further exists, accompanied and supported in some way by the act of Judas, his betrayal, his remorse, and his Cord, this same Work became efficacious on earth, for it thus gave a new orientation to all humanity, spilling Satan redeemed into the very blood of Mankind.

At that moment, the Angle of the Baseline was formed, and the horizontal line of the Triangle to which we belong was virtually drawn. The Second Era was commencing.

O disciple! If you cannot penetrate this mystery, if you cannot understand this dogma, which explains what the Man did more than nineteen centuries ago, to pacify the struggle between the Yes and the No and to orient the divine forces in the direction of Satan Redeemed, if you need palpable proof of this teaching transmitted by the Invisible Masters who are still hidden because the hour of their triumph has not yet sounded, if you cannot admit anything but what has been weighed and measured—leave this place and take your footsteps elsewhere.

Here, in the Court of the Knights of the Golden Arrow, where the young Sweepers boldly and patiently clean up the dusty heritage that has been left to us by our ancestors, grown old upon the long roads, the first faith is strictly required.

Faith is transmitted contagiously. It emanates from the Master, and it touches the student or not.

If you are not touched by this grace, depart.

If you at least wish to be touched by it, stay yet and wait.

Behold the three torches lit in our Temple: the torch of

The Holy of Holies

Reason, the torch of the Heart, and the torch of Sex.*

The torch of Reason is dim in the skeptic. It is luminous in the head of the man who has faith. It permits the latter to formulate and to articulately transmit to others what he himself has learned.

The skeptic is limited. He does not grasp the deep sense of things, because he does not wish to fix his attention on anything other than the exterior surfaces. The deep reality escapes him because of this.

We shall not keep within the confines of this Court the skeptics whose narrowness of spirit is incurable. These people will never understand in what way they belong to the Universe. They are the dead branches, harmful to the health of the human tree, and the new current will not bring them into the Third Era.

We shall only keep with us those individuals who are capable of believing, after having long contemplated the Infinite and the Impalpable. They are the ones whose Heart torch is alight.

The first two torches are indispensable for the lighting of the third: the torch of Sex, whose radiation is immense and its magical power limitless.

No one shall cross the threshold of the Holy of Holies alive, the threshold of the Tabernacle where the Rod of Fecundation

---

*[These three represent the three apices of the Triangle, which correspond to the beginning points of the eras of Judaism, Christianity, and the new religion of the Third Term of the Trinity. —*Trans.*]

mutely rests in the Ark of Formation, and no one shall know the Name of God, if the Light of Sex does not illuminate him and fortify him with its sublime fire, at last permitting him to see the Unknown.

Those who have this Light are the true circumcised, for they have received the second kiss of Satan, the second bite of the Symbolic Serpent, whose baptism is definitive.

AFTER DEATH

O disciple! There is no longer anything for you beyond death!

Your life ends with your last breath.

Your conscience shines forth when you come into the world; it disappears irremediably at your death.

No one continues to light a broken lamp, and a leaf detached from the branch does not take up again its place on the Tree of Life.

What is dead, is dead definitively.

It is so that you should not forget this truth that we have embroidered the head of a dry cadaver upon your Sweeper shirt. And you will not be admitted to the tests of the second degree as long as it has not become dear to you.

For you will be happy one day—if you persevere—to know that your life has an end, because you will truly and deeply understand that the division is the essential error. The error of God (= Life) and not your own.

Ah! If you were able to no longer live in yourself and for yourself, if it were possible for you to reunite in your consciousness all of the consciousnesses dispersed throughout the world, if your thought could be the thought of all and your feeling the feeling of all, if all humanity were truly concentrated in you, then, yes, you could have been immortal. But then you would be Life (=God) and you would have acted like It: you would have fought against Satan.

The result of it would then have been what you already know: the fragmentation of the centers of power, the individualization of the stars and of their systems, the differentiation among species and races, the isolation, such as you see it, of the human consciousness.

And what you would have divided and multiplied would have received, as you are already aware, the satanic will of the Adversary of God (= Life), which tends to the reunion and reunification of the whole universe in the sole, unique Spirit where all is reduced to Nothingness.

Understand something here: if the infinite could be reduced to zero, Satan would long ago have triumphed. But because the infinite goes beyond zero, the work of the unifying Adversary is irremediably condemned to imperfection.

Satan will tend unceasingly toward the impossible vertical,* but he will always fall into the sinuosities of the horizontal.†

---

*[Unmanifested reunion with the Divine. —_Trans._]
†[Material existence in the visible world. —_Trans._]

Meanwhile, precisely because it is impossible, the total realization of the Work* of Satan† will be eternally wished for.

It will be wished for in all of Nature, in each plant, in each animal, and in all humans.

In some it will manifest itself in a chaotic fashion, in others in a brutal way. But if you remain here, and if you persuade yourself of the truth of our Doctrine, you will lead it with order and method to the maximum of its possible perfection.

In that way you will also prove your quality as a civilized person who knows how to build.

You will know, in addition, that it is just and good that you should not be immortal; that it is just and good that you should die irremediably, after having done whatever you could during your short existence on this earth that would most benefit the Work of Satan,‡ and to benefit the correction of his Protestation brought incessantly to the chaotic Work of the division and the multiplication of Life (= God).

But you will render to the flesh that which belongs to it:

You will nourish yourself;

You will care for your body;

You will reproduce yourself.

Your work being necessarily imperfect, it is necessary that in

---

*[Transcendence of what is material and manifest. —*Trans.*]

†[Here "Satan" represents the will to physical death and non-manifestation. —*Trans.*]

‡[As explained above, this work is essentially the transcendence of manifested existence in order to reunite with the divine. —*Trans.*]

and by your posterity you should still continue the same effort toward the impossible goal.

This is why you will have one or several children, and you will give them the best education possible, in order to in turn make of them civilized persons, capable of affirming the satanic* architecture in the natural chaos of animal man.

You will apply yourself to create your immortality in your posterity and, more broadly, in the generations that will follow your own.

O disciple! No immortality has been granted you, save that which you can gain in the memory of men.

Make the effort to conquer this immortality.

It is much more real than you may believe today.

Jesus of Nazareth is living, he is really immortal and always active—even if he never existed!—because his memory is imperishable.

But it takes a great work, an immense heroism, to consolidate the memory of a man in the generations that follow.

It is necessary that this work should contain a profound human (satanic and divine) truth, and it is necessary that it should coincide with the will of the Hour, marked on the dial written in the Triangle to which one belongs.

Now today we are still in the shadow of the Second Night of our Triangle.

The new Sun is scarcely born in the shadows that envelop

---

*[The will to transcendence of the physical manifestation. —_Trans._]

us, and the Divine Mother, Humanity, is giving birth.

Do you not hear her piercing cries, do you not see the blood that flows from her insides?

The work of the present Hour is that of the midwife.

The one who today will be the great midwife, abling, aiding in the birth of the New Man, that one will be immortal, because future generations will not forget him.

There are already those who understand what must be done and consequently act.

Be one of their number, and inscribe on your forehead the sign of the New Man.

He is called the Liberated One.

He has traversed the storm of the Second Era, but neither steel nor fire have been able to harm him.

The Son, at the same time, of the Crucified and of the Hanged, he venerates both, and renders hommage to them.

He loves Humanity—his Daughter and his Mother—and he is full of solicitude for her.

He will reign over the whole earth, for he is worthy of reigning, and the peoples will obey him with joy and trust.

He comes for all peoples and all races, but he will replace each leaf upon its branch, for only the trunk and the root are common to all.

The reign of the New Man is already commencing, for he is the new Sun, who is being born now in the shadows of the Second Night.

His blossoming will be triumphal on the next Noon, but

at the decline of the Third Day, he will reenter the shadows, as the sun does every evening. Then there will be a new Master Horseman in the invisible regions, while Humanity will begin again, upon the line of the Fall, a new Triangle . . . under other skies, with other blood.

We have explained this necessity in *The Light of Sex.*

THE MAGNIFICENT
INVISIBLE KNIGHTS

H e who dares to speak of the Magnificent Invisible Knights dares much, because the greatest mystery surrounds them.

Not because of their pretended unreality, but because of the irreducible imperfection of the child-persons who people this earth.

The child-person of the twentieth century of the Second Era of our Triangle does not conceive of anything other than what he can compare to himself, as he is or as he would like to be. That which is totally different from him seems to him to be nonexistent.

That is why it is dangerous to speak to him of the Magnificent Invisible Knights, whose characteristic is precisely to be different from those who, on this earth, would like to know them.

At the same time, no initiation could be sufficient without this Marvelous Chapter, and since the minister of public initiation has so ordered us, we shall here summarize what we can say about it.

One should read these pages with attention, while rejecting any spirit of idolatry.*[1]

Comparison leads to idolatry, and the latter shuns the incomparable.

Do not be idolaters, do not compare.

Do not judge either, for you are incapable of it.

Accept or reject in its totality the teaching that is given to you.

If you cannot accept it and you don't even want to reject it, because it attracts you, try to acquire interior eyes and ears, only by means of which you would be able to understand and, consequently, sincerely accept our Word.

But the acquisition of the new qualities requires the sacrifice of those that you have at this moment and which you need for the defense of your daily existence. Decide then to suffer, if you wish to acquire the higher qualities.

Can you do it? Would you be capable of begging in the sumptuous streets of your capitals? Would you have the courage to confront the scorn of your contemporaries without weakening?

Everything is there, in that courage. If you have it, come to us. If not, follow the beaten paths, but do not be surprised if others pass you up.

---

*[Naglowska uses this admonition as a shorthand way of reminding us not to imagine "Satan" as living outside of ourselves. —*Trans.*]

No human being has a special right to initiation, nor even to understanding. Human rights are limited to the average qualities, which help to live in peace on this earth, that is to say to enjoy more or less reasonably the goods of this world.

Knowledge, and even simply understanding, are privileges that one acquires at the cost of a hard struggle, which would not be able to be eased under any circumstance.

Neither because of human weakness, nor because of their good will, nor because of their human kindness.

And it is not, anyway, necessary that the initiates should be numerous.

Man was not made for initiation into the great Mysteries, but for laborious drudgery in this lower world.

He who liberates himself from slavery, to which he has been destined, is a rebel; and nothing, in the Universe, wishes rebellion.

Only Satan preaches revolt, but Satan* is the Adversary of the Universe.

He does not call anyone, but he glides, like a serpent, through the wild moss and caresses with his venomous tongue the one whom he has chosen.

In the fortunate victim a new fire is lighted then.

---

*[This "Satan," which is the will to die, is opposed to physical manifestation. When redeemed or reconciled, it will become a drive toward spiritualization and transcendence of the physical. —*Trans.*]

Initiation into the great Mysteries, as all true understanding, begins with the first kiss of Satan.*

If you want this kiss because of the joy that it brings, leave your comfortable houses and prostrate yourselves in the moss.

The latter is humid in the nocturnal hours, and the enemies of Man are numerous in the forests.

Have you the courage to bear the thousand wounds of all the insects and all the wild beasts, determined to harm you because you scorn the order that they represent and because you want a glory that passes them up?

Satanic joy,† the true joy in the bosom of the Only Light, comes at this price.

Reflect on it well, weigh the pros and cons, before deciding.

The path that we are pointing out to you is full of dangerous thorns, and one does not come back if one starts out on it.

There is no hurry, anyway, and if you do not come another will come in your place.

I, you, or another, it is the same anonymity, for the NAME is a single one and its hour has not yet sounded.

For now, here is what you must learn, before accepting or rejecting.

Each time that a historic Triangle ends, because the three

---

*[Without claiming and reconciling this "dark side," our understanding of life is necessarily incomplete. — *Trans.*]

†[The joy that has accepted and reconciled dark and light, death and life. — *Trans.*]

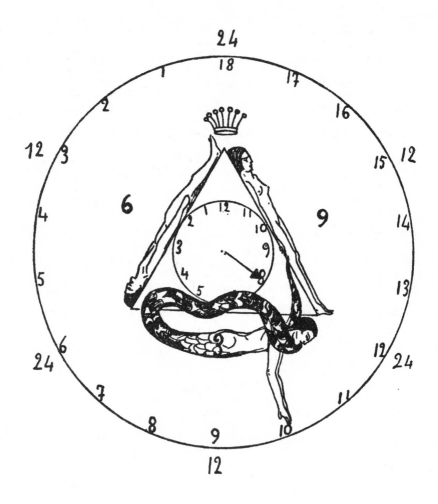

The Cosmic Clock

lines that compose it—the line of the Fall, the line of the Struggle, and that of the Triumph, characterized respectively by the Rod, the Cross, and the Arrow, and successively bearing the torches of the Father (Reason), the Son (the Heart), and the Mother (Sex)— have been followed by the Humanity that elaborates them, a new Master-Knight is formed.

He is in a way the flower, or the quintessence, of the Tree of Life, come to this term, or, to say it better, to this age.

He is the goal of the work accomplished by all, through the centuries and the generations, through three long Cosmic Days, and through the First and Second Nights.

It is he, of whom it is secretly said that he has been born four times.

The first time, at the Dawn of the Triangle, which determines the Fall.

The second time, in the First deep Night, where the Crucifixion is accomplished, followed by the Second Bite of the Symbolic Serpent.

The third time, in the heart of the Second Night, during which is effected the laborious birthing of the New Man.

The fourth time, on the re-attained summit of the Triangle, since "the first things have passed."

He is therefor the Blazing Star, of which the points are five and the rays innumerable.

The first three points are three heads, three Cosmic Days; and the other two points are the two living columns, one black and the other white, by means of which Man raises himself above the banks that border the red river of animal life.*

The innumerable rays are the innumerable phosphorescences that are released by everyone and everything.

The Blazing Star is the Crown of Humanity: this is why the Magnificent Invisible Knights are truly powerful Kings.

The power is not given to them, but it is acquired by them by the collective effort of all of Humanity, through all generations and all centuries of a given Triangle.

What do they do with their power?

Certainly not what some mortal men would do. And if someone comes along to tell you that they do this or that, as judges or as human leaders, don't believe it.

The activity of He who is the Goal is not that of those who are the path.

You are the path, you cannot understand that which is the Destination.

If you were on the path and not the path itself, perhaps you would be able to imagine, approximately, of what the Destination is composed.

If you were on the path and not the path itself, there would already be in you, in some fashion, the first indications of the Goal. You would have the first elements of it, the first nature, and one could have said of you that you were the beginning of it.

But you have nothing in you of that which will be the End Purpose.

---

*[This is an important passage, containing an important image, and we'll have occasion to refer to it several times. —*Trans.*]

You are all fundamentally attached to the earth, to its needs, to its servitudes.

You have been condemned to this slavery since the beginning of the Triangle, to which you belong and the three lines of which you form successively—the line of the Fall, that of the Struggle, and that of the Triumph—and it is impossible for you to subtract yourself from what you are.

Do not believe that you are all attached to a chain or that you are dragging one. No, you are the chain itself, and you can't be anything other than what you are.

It is well that you are kept from knowing what the Goal will be, the Blazing Star, whose triumph will be great at the last moment, since the third line of the Triangle, the line that we are beginning today, will reach its end, rejoining the beginning of the new Fall.

And so it is this that keeps you from understanding of what the activity of those is composed, who are of a kind of Stars in the sky whose vision is forbidden to you.

Human words and human comparisons cannot translate their acts, because the qualities that they possess are too different from those that characterize mortal men of the earth.

In the human sense, they are neither good, nor just, nor patient, nor even attentive; and nothing of what is done down here by individuals—the leaves attached to the branches—can interest them, for, coming from the whole of the people who have formed them, only the whole is their origin and their succession.

The last "whole" that formed the last Magnificent Knight

was his Mother and his cradle, and the whole that has developed since, through the new Triangle, is preparing the birth of his new Brother.

It is only in this sense that Humanity interests him.

The Marvelous Chapter of the Invisible Knights directs the march of historical events, with the only aim of favoring the birth of the new Star "at the end of times," that is to say at the instant of the closing of the current Triangle.

If this did not interest the Marvelous chapter, the latter would not occupy itself with us at all, and then, no one on earth would perceive the least echo of it.

At the same time, there are occasionally some who do hear the strange Voice, the astonishing Chant, coming from one knows not where.

There are some who submit to the invincible spell and who suddenly pronounce strange words.

The profane mock these people and treat them as lost souls, believing that they are raving. But those who observe them closely soon realize that they enjoy exceptional protection.

In effect, they feed themselves little or not at all, but they keep all of their strength.*

They are persecuted and resented, but they remain serene.

One inflicts sufferings upon them, but they do not suffer.

They seem crushed by adversities of all sorts, but their good humor shines forth just the same.

---

*[Naglowska must here have had herself in mind, because this is a good description of the way she lived. —*Trans.*]

Incontestably, they are stronger and richer than the others, but if you ask them where their riches are, they will make a vague gesture and will tell you "elsewhere."

For, certainly, they themselves are *elsewhere,* if they know what the shining Members of the Unknown Fraternity are, the Members of the Marvelous Chapter, whose impalpable Breath they have felt.

They are no longer the road formed by the leaves, but new pathways.

They are no longer passive links in the long and heavy chain, but they are new fingers that lift up this chain.

They no longer run, like some soft and ignorant drops that do not know where the currents are taking them, but they are a new mist, imbued with higher radiations.

They are those of whom it is said that they follow the Voice that calls in the dry desert, sown with sand that is deaf and mute.

And because they are *something else,* they no longer care about the petty human troubles and vain ambitions of the proud and weak.

And, adapting themselves perfectly to the exigencies of the historical Hours, marked upon the dial written in the living Triangle, they teach, act, or are silent.

Officially or not according to circumstances, they always belong to the great, true Brotherhood of the Knights of the Golden Arrow.

THE LAST ORAL
EXAMINATION BEFORE
THE GREAT TEST

The great initiatic test of Hanging is preceded by a last oral examination in the course of which the Master measures the physical, moral, and spiritual strength of the candidate.

Here is what one reads in one of the protocols, bringing together the different phases of such a test:

The Master: Here you are in your turn on this bench where so many others, before you, have come to sit with the same hope, perhaps with the same courage. You have seen some of them leave here. Some were afflicted, others left joyfully; for those of the second group imagined that their answers had been perfectly correct. Now, my brother, an answer may be sufficient, but it can never be perfect, for no one can have an adequate idea of Truth, because the latter is never what it will be tomorrow. Can you stop a star at a given point in its trajectory and say that in a thousand years, at point mn,* it will be the same? Truth is living, my brother, and like Life, it changes incessantly. On the one hand, it is subjected to certain laws by its past, and on the other, it creates the future. There is therefore in it a constant factor, which you can know completely, if such is your degree of understanding, and an unforeseeable factor, which is called the Unknown. This is why if you prophesize you take the part of the uncertain . . . And now, let us get on with our examination. From where do you come?

The candidate: I was born in the red river of the animal kingdom. My memories begin there. I had then, like everybody, the age that is numbered by three. Like everybody, I was a slave and, like everybody, I did not know it. Still, on the dial of the great Universal Clock, the twelfth hour was beginning, and circumstances, of which I was not the master, pushed me along a dark road, in a country whose name I did not know. There, I wandered for a long time with neither fire nor light, but I grew and attained seven years. I returned then to the town of my birth, but there was no longer anything in common between me and mine. I spoke a language

---

*[Is it only coincidence that these coordinates are Naglowska's initials? Probably not, since more than once she seemed to identify herself with the "Morning Star." —*Trans.*]

that no one understood and I had dreams that seemed crazy. This was the most painful period of my life, because around me I saw only sick people, who did not wish to become well. I had the cure, they did not accept it. One day my despair was at its height, and it was then that a woman said to me, "You are still too close to them, that is why they don't understand you. Depart from here once more, find the castle of your dreams, study its architecture and its technical construction, and then come back to build your town here, without asking the advice of anyone. When they see that your town is beautiful and comfortable, they will listen to you, without asking the least explanation of you, and if you wish to be their king, they will crown you." The woman went away, and I came here.

The Master: "Have you found what you hoped for here?"

The candidate: "I have lost here even the memory of what I wanted, for I have learned a new wisdom."

The Master: "What have you learned?"

The candidate: "Essentially this: one cannot give people anything, if the hour for the gift has not sounded."

The Master: "Who sounds the hour?"

The candidate: "The will of the person who wills this."

The Master: "Do you will it?"

The candidate: "No."

The Master: "Do you wish to acquire the will?"

The candidate: "No."

The Master: "Do you believe that, if you had wished it, you would have been able to acquire it here?"

The candidate: "No."

The Master: "But then what are you doing in this Temple?"

The candidate: "I am waiting."

The Master: "Do you wish to tell me what you are waiting for?"

The candidate: "I am waiting for the promised baptism, my third birth, because I have determined that each time that I get older, a new desire is born in me. My first birth in the red river gave me some appetites. My second birth, in the unknown country, gave me, in adding four years, the desire to raise others to my own level. The wisdom that I have acquired here, in the course of my time in the Court of the Sweepers, and in the tests of the second degree, have made of me a Freedman, who has a single desire: to be Him, the rejected Spirit in the meanders of Hell and whose liberation depends on my success. Here is a program: I will present myself for the test, which, if all goes well, will precipitate in me, from high to low, the Dark Element, which is called Satan. I will be Him then, the Disapproved, projected into

Humanity since the beginning of our Triangle. I will look at my Fiancée, *My Mother and My Daughter,* and if I awaken in Her the love that I wish, the Victory will be mine, and all things will become new, because in Her and through Her, everything will be changed. Then, there will no longer be either weeping or gnashing of teeth, because the New Man will be born, and he will know how and be capable of doing what he already wishes."

The Master: "And if you fail?"

The candidate: "I will crawl on the humid earth, like a hated serpent, and I will not find refuge or joy anywhere."

The Master: "You say that with a very calm voice. Are you so sure of succeeding?"

The candidate: "I have protected my heart with a solid shield, and I have put my thoughts in order. What must happen to me will happen!"

The Master: "I have noted your answers and your reflections on this parchment. My brother, you may leave. The great test will take place tomorrow."

THE PRIESTESSES
OF LOVE

A sacred text, the origin of which is lost in the night of time, reveals this:

One will know, but one will not understand, that the priestess of love is a virgin.

"One will learn, but one will not believe, that virginity is the great satanic* virtue—the No holding power in her deep fortress—which determines in the woman the special charm and the captivating magic of which she will make use at hour 'twelve'† to crush the head of the Serpent and to lead onto the Path of Life the Purified Rebel, the shadowy Satan, now become Light.

"Nor will one admit, since this is opposed to the easy pleasure of the perverse man, that the male principle brings death

*[Because it is opposed to physical manifestation. —*Trans.*]
†[On the Cosmic Clock. —*Trans.*]

The Woman and the Serpent

to the female principle, each time that a man teaches a woman how to take pleasure there where she should remain ever passive and unknowing.

"For joy belongs to the sun and it is proper to the sun, while the mysterious mount of the woman is essentially lunar, and, like the moon, it should remain cold and mute.

"The vibrations of the woman, at the moment of the act of love, should give her happiness and not localized pleasure, for the pleasure belongs to the man and not to the woman.

"Disgrace enters into human generations when men depart from this truth, teaching women that which they should never know: localized pleasure.

"Women age rapidly when they bite into this forbidden fruit, and the blood of their children becomes impoverished . . .

"But the priestesses of love shall be virgins: they will not know the forbidden fruit.

"One will choose them from among young women whom the sun has not corrupted, from among women whose dreams are pure as the moon and who themselves are like harps, all of whose strings vibrate and sing when the able fingers of the artist plucks them one by one, to extract a melody from them.

"One will bathe them, like precious plants, in sweet and perfumed water, and one will care for their skin by means of aromatic essences, wisely prepared according to the tested formulas of the Mages.

"One will watch with solicitude so that no evil spell should be cast upon the priestesses-in-training by profane approaches, in order that their growth should not deviate and their development should be protected from all morbid problems.

"One will not impose upon them any work that could be harmful to the harmony of their bodies, and one will strictly forbid them any pose or attitude that is unaesthetic.

"The priestesses of love will be exposed regularly to the propitious action of the lunar rays from the first to the fifteenth night of each lunar month.

"The young priestesses will then form nocturnal processions and circles, singing refrains that stir the spirit. The older ones will take part in more advanced dances, to the rhythm of tunes composed by the Mages.

"During the hours of midday heat, when the sun's action is particularly strong, the priestesses in training will rest in their common room, the curtains of which will all be lowered. The Mage assigned to their education, sitting in the middle of the room, will oversee the order and calm necessary to safeguard the purity of the feminine principle; and, when the women have plunged into deep sleep, accentuated by his influence, the Mage will orient the dreams of the priestesses toward such goal as he shall deem useful.

"Each hour marked on the dial of the Universal Clock has its purpose and meaning. The Mages know that and conform themselves to it.

"At dusk, the Mage will awaken the women and will question them about the content of their dreams. He will give them the necessary explanations and will converse with them on

The Sacred Dances

subjects that could awaken in them the desire to fly to more worthy regions.

"For the priestesses of love are destined to prepare the future of humanity. Their role is not to concern themselves with what is happening in profane society, which follows its destiny determined by the past, but to cultivate interior consciousness, and to watch over the holy flame that illuminates the new paths.

"Woe to the peoples and races who shall not have, when the time comes, their nursery of priestesses of love! Woe to those men who shall forget the holy mission of the Woman and shall no longer have, in their temples, the burning mystic light without which humanity cannot overcome its evils.

"A terrible epoch awaits humanity at midnight of the Second Night. The Beast will then come out from the bottom of the sea and furiously set upon all the children of the earth. The temples will be profaned and, in the towns and villages, women will give themselves to prostitution. Atrocious diseases will be the portion of men, and their intelligence will quickly decline. There will be wars and bloody revolutions, and no one will any longer know where Truth lies.

"But at the last minute, and when the pain is at its peak, a woman will proclaim openly where the plagues and calamities are coming from. She will place her foot upon the head of the Serpent and extract from its unclean mouth the tail that it has been biting for so long. Then the Light of Sex will shine forth and peace will return to the human spirit. Order will be reestablished among the unaware. They will reconstruct the Temple of the Third Era, and there they will light the three Torches of Wisdom: The Torch of Reason, that of the Heart, and that of Sex. What is sacred will then be respected, and Humanity will be happy until the next Evening . . ."

This text contains—as any can verify who know how to read—the original inspiration, which pierces the tangled skein of all real religions having served as the basis for human civilzations.

Judaism and, after it, Christianity have stressed and retained this very promise of salvation brought by a woman, when human disgrace is no longer bearable, because of the diverse and terrible ills that it will engender.

But, while the official religions of our centuries have applied themselves to the hiding of the true sense of this prophesy, in order not to hasten the march of events, the Brotherhood of the Knights of the Golden Arrow has kept the purity of its meaning intact.

That is why the young women, secretly entrusted to the influence of the invisible chapels of these Noble Warriors, are still today the rare candles crowned with sacred initiatic fire, by contact with which the Third Torch of Humanity, the healing Torch of holy and wholesome Sex, will be able to be relit.

This solemn event is near, and the chosen are hastening even now before the Bride whose wedding will consecrate the beginning of the New Era by the joyous celebration of the Golden Mass.

Yet a little patience, still some tears and some gnashing of teeth, and the Lie that gnaws on the head of the Serpent (*human reason*)* will be effaced. For at the Dawn the dew rises and it puts to flight the malefic shadows of the Night.

Today it is still impossible to tell all of the truth, because not all of the malefactors have been punished. There are those who keep the appearance of power and use it to maintain on earth the false day of artificial light, so that the Dawn is confused and the first rays of the Rising Sun are pale and timid.

But soon their death will be definitive. The rebirth of the good will precipitate the bad into the depths of the primitive animal regions, and no one else will be able to trouble the ascendant march of Humanity toward the final goal, where the Blazing Star of the Morning will shine joyfully.

Woe to those who oppose this inescapable realization!

Woe to the perverse and perfidious men who, with their vile smile and their lips bathed in abject drivel, still prevent the holy sacrifice of the Golden Mass.

It is because of them that the hour of the redemption of humanity is delayed and sufferings of all kinds are prolonged.

It is they, those sordid beings who call themselves men but in truth are nothing more than foul vipers, unworthy to tread the soil of the *other shore,* who delay the happy crossing of the bridge before which Humanity has been pawing the earth for

---

*[This is Naglowska's gloss, not the translator's. —*Trans.*]

more than a century, while sinking further and further into the humid clay of the rotten bank.

Those men pretend that they possess the light, but it is not true, for their reason is one of the daughters of the shadows.

They say that they bring justice and well-being for all, but they lie, for their appetites are ferocious, and they act like ogres, who promise much only to then devour the sheep caught in their snares.

All of those men must die as they deserve to, so that there may be light.

Then they will be thrown into the bowels of the earth, from which the return is slow and painful through innumerable Triangles, in accordance with the laws of Wisdom.

Then, in the rose-colored chapels, decorated with flowers and burning candles, the women, initiated into the sublime mystery of the Triumph, will pour out upon all those present the benefic influence of their radiance.

But today, this is still not possible, because the men and women who compose the crowds are not capable of admitting the merit of what surpasses their understanding. They still do not know, and do not understand, that while the one deserving is a single one, in him and through him all share in the recompense.

And because the profane do not know that, and combat, instead of supporting, those who surpass them in understanding and wisdom, the priestesses, entrusted to the influence of the Golden Arrow, surround their ministry with impenetrable secrecy, in such a way that, until the last minute, no one knows where the rite (whose description we will give further on) will take place, nor the name or other details about the woman whose true testimony we now cite:

"I saw him, pale and panting, wounded by a terrible weapon.

"Without doubt, he was going to die or finish his days lamentably, in some lost corner of the earth.

"His legs barely supported him, and his death rattle was atrocious.

"He moved forward in the thick forest, leaning on the trunks of the trees, and when I lost him from view I found him again by following the bloody traces that his hands left on the brown bark.

"I begged him to stop, but he fled from me like a hunted beast, full of fear.

"'But I have only good intentions with regard to you,' I said to him, having walked behind him for a long time. 'Are you afraid of me? What harm could I do to you?'

"Much farther on, and when he could do no more, he answered me:

"'No one can do anything, either for good or ill, for the man who has sustained defeat. You are wasting your time following me, for the dying belong to the dead and the reborn to the living. Go back home and let me die.'

"He was weary. He sank to the moss.

"'I'm staying near you, if you don't mind,' I said to him. 'I have plenty of time, I assure you, and no one waits for me under any roof. I recognize you by your clothes, which are those of a Hunter of the Golden Arrow, and I can easily imagine what combat you have succumbed to. I will not tarnish your honor with paltry pity, for if you have been vanquished it does not necessarily mean that you have lacked courage. I have seen some stronger than you hide the same sorrow deep in this forest and reject, as you are doing at this moment, my will to help. The hardiest can do nothing, if the hour of Victory has not sounded; but if no one falls, the Struggle cannot end. I am here to render homage to you, O superb sacrificial victim.'

"'I thank you for it,' he said in a very weak voice. 'I see that you understand the Doctrine. So you know, and it is useless for me to repeat it to you, that for me everything is finished. I don't feel bad about it. The lamp that I am is extinguished. Another, somewhere else, will be lit. Go and say good-bye to my Brothers, and remember me, if your heart tells you to.'

"This speech had worn him out. He stretched out at full length and closed his eyes. Was he dead? Would he be revived?

"Then I did what the Rule prescribes for priestesses consoling the defeated. Slowly, I drew around the injured man the gestures and the steps that compress the emanations of the dying body and, when the isolating wall vibrated at a meter's distance around, calculated from the solar plexus of the stretched-out Hunter, I knelt near him, taking care that I was in the center of the fluid enclosure.

"Immediately bending over the defeated man, I threw open

the fabrics that veiled his skin below my head. I poured out on his body, from the waist to the beginning of his legs, the perfume that I carried (as do all of our sisters) in the folds of my green silk waistband, and when his skin had absorbed the perfume, I poured out on the abdomen of the dying man the flood of my blond hair.

"While I did these things, to aid his death or his rebirth, I murmured the prayer that we chant at the March full moon:

> *"As you wish to be reborn, earth, welcome*
> *   him!*
> *"As you wish to melt, ice, respect him!*
> *"As you wish to shine and to rejoice, sun,*
> *   look upon him!*
> *"As you do not wish to die, shadows,*
> *   transform yourselves!*

"I was repeating these verses for the third time when, suddenly, the miracle happened: he who seemed dead or at the point of death, sat up, so brusquely that my head was wedged solidly into the angle formed by his seated body. The Hunter rested his palms on the nape of my neck to prevent me from rising, and I heard him breathe deeply of the fresh air.

"'He is coming back to life,' I said to myself, so his injury was not mortal!

"I stayed still, without the least movement, in order not to disturb his rebirth.

"He still kept his hands on the nape of my neck, but his breathing was becoming normal again. Suddenly, he said this to me:

"'I know now that all of that was nothing more than a stage set, a pretext for breaking my pride. It is now that my true life starts, for everything that has happened until this was nothing more than a faint sketch . . . a preparation . . . a first attempt.'

"He said, then, in a stronger voice:

"'Woman, sit up and look into my eyes, for you are my Mother and I am your son, and I wish to receive my new name from your lips.'

"He removed his fingers from my tangled hair, and I sat up to obey him. I looked into his eyes and I saw that his face really was new.

"I gave him the name that he carries now, but which no one may know except his Mother, your sister who writes this, and the Venerable Warriors, his Brothers, for a new name is a new essence, and those who do not yet have it or will never have it cannot conceive of it . . .

"The reception of the new Warrior into the midst of the family of the Invisibles was celebrated the next day, at night-fall. I was elevated to the grade of Venerable Mother, because he could have died but instead he became my son by the secret virtue of recognition.

"Glory and salvation to all those who understand this Mystery."

9

THE RITE OF
HANGING

The sacred rite of the Hanging is the great initiatic test, to which the Freed Hunters of the Brotherhood of the Golden Arrow submit themselves, upon their return from their voyage into the profane world, which is imposed upon them after the ceremony of the Virile Taper, the description of which we have given in *The Light of Sex*.

The voyage of the Freedman can last three years, seven years, or even twelve years; but the Hunter who does not return after that extreme delay is no longer accepted among the Brotherhood and, in the chapel of the priestesses, his lamp is then extinguished before his portrait.

Because it is said in the sacred books:

"He who has passed the test of the second degree has his eyes and ears open when he goes back to the milieu of the crowds. Because of that, he runs the great danger of becoming intoxicated with his power, which the profane admire and flatter because they see its concrete results. The purest quickly see that, and they return to the enclosure of the Satanic*[1] Temple after three years of voyage. Others, less well "cleansed," profit from the permission that is given them to prolong their sojourn in the profane world for seven years or even twelve years; but, when they show themselves here for the Great Test, it is quite rare for them to be successful. For it is difficult to conquer pride that has become a thick shell."

And also, in a book "for the women," one reads this:

"The priestess whose Beloved shall have succumbed to the Hanging Test, after having tried in vain to heal him, will come back to the Temple, with eyelids lowered and heart troubled by shame. Before the Areopagus, which shall meet for this purpose, she will declare the failure of her Fiancé, and the priestesses, her sisters, will cover her with red and black veils under which she shall be hidden from that time on and until her death.

"In a funereal procession, the women will take themselves to their chapel, and the 'widow' will proceed to the extinction of the lamp over whose holy and wholesome flame she had watched since her Lover's test of the Virile Taper (see *The Light of Sex*).

---

*[It is called that because the Brotherhood strives to counterbalance "the red river of animal life" (see chapters 6 and 7) with a transcendent, spiritual existence. "Satan" here represents opposition to manifested physical existence. The "Satanic Temple" cannot be a place where a "Satan" is worshipped, both because there is no such worship in Naglowska's system and because she has forbidden her followers to imagine "Satan" as something living outside of ourselves, a practice, which she considers to be idolatry. Naglowska's use of "Satanic" in her symbolic language was (probably intentionally) misleading; "Temple of Transcendence" would have been a better term. —*Trans.*]

"The priestesses, her sisters, will immediately take her to the door of the pavilion of the 'widows,' which she will never leave again, except in the dark hours of nights without moonlight, during which the mysterious rounds of the women in mourning will take place, whose obstinate hope surpasses human comprehension.

"No Mage, no Warrior or Freed Hunter shall approach these sorrowful women under pain of death; and whoever shall have come upon their macabre chants will have an incurable wound upon his body. For what is dead belongs to Death, and what is living belongs to Life, and if you confuse the Future with the Past, you throw confusion into the paths where building is to be done."

The Test of Hanging begins at eight o'clock in the evening.

From dawn to dusk on this day, seven Venerable Warriors and twelve witnesses chosen from among the Mages and their most knowledgeable disciples, prepare themselves with special care for the terrible "encounter," of which the issue is most often tragic.

They proceed to make frequent, aromatic ablutions, which coat their skin from head to toe with isolating creams, whose formulas are individual for each one.

They nourish themselves with fruits and wheat crêpes every three hours and, in the interval between meals, they remain silent, stretched out upon carpets arranged for their use in the lower meditation chamber.

This room is laid out in the basement, exactly beneath the main arena of the Temple, and from the latter it gets its circular shape.

A curtain of gray silk follows the curve of the wall at a distance of about three-quarters of a meter from it, forming a passage so narrow that it would be difficult for two to walk abreast.

The fruits, the wheat crêpes, the fresh water, and the isolating perfumes and creams have been disposed upon low tables, in the middle of the room, since the beginning of their vigil by the Warriors and Mages themselves; for no one has the right to come under this roof, either by day or by night, except the Venerables of the third degree of Satanic* Initiation, the Mages and their advanced disciples, because of the vampiric fluids distributed through the atmosphere of this windowless room.

The nature of these fluids is such that in a matter of seconds they suck out the blood of mortals insufficiently armed to resist them, and one cites, in the Annals of the Brotherhood of the Golden Arrow, the case of a young Sweeper who, having disobeyed out of curiosity, or perhaps, to serve the curiosity of some indiscreet questioner, was found dead in the middle of the room, a quarter of an hour after his entry into it.

Other stories are told, still more lugubrious, but those are

---

*[Again, in Naglowska's symbolic language this term signifies the Will to Die, as opposed to the Will to Live, and therefore also opposition to manifested physical existence, and a hoped-for spiritual transcendence of the physical. —*Trans.*]

not verified or verifiable, because they were not officially registered, for reasons that I don't know.

One assures us, for example, that a very beautiful young woman was found, one day, on a rug of the lower room, immobile and like a wax doll, draped in transparent blue and yellow veils. The College of the Mages was alerted right away by the two Warriors who found this woman, and the worthy old gentlemen descended in their turn, with uneasy air and grave faces. When the Healer-Mage had pronounced the customary conjuration in order to send away from the stretched-out body the force of the Shadows, which were sucking on it no doubt, the veils that covered the young woman faded and were reabsorbed into the carpet, taking with them in their dissolution the corpse, too. The carpet kept the imprint of the beautiful creature for nearly a hundred and forty-four years, and the Mages and the Brotherhood of the Golden Arrow made use of it for operations whose meaning, purpose, and keys only they knew . . .

The seven Venerable Warriors and the twelve advanced disciples silently prepare the test of the Freed Hunter, who desires to pass through the rite of Hanging to the grade of Warrior; and the fifteen hours, which they spend stretched out in the dangerous lower meditation room serve them to test their own strength.

If a weakness, even of the slightest, is produced in the spirit or the body of one of them, the others soothe and comfort him, recharging him with the force that he is lacking. But most often these worthy men support the day of reclusion in the lower room without the least trouble of any kind, and when, at eight o'clock in the evening, the Chief gives the signal, they all rise as one and arrange themselves in a circle to receive the Freedman who is to be tested.

The latter, entirely covered by a dense, hooded robe of violet silk, slowly descends the steps of the spiral staircase, which starts at the main arena of the Temple, and ends in the narrow passage formed by the gray curtain and the round wall of the lower room.

He advances like a blind man, and certainly the unknown route must seem longer to him than it is. He obeys the order that is given him by the guide, when the latter, at eight o'clock, opens the door to the spiral staircase in front of him and says to him, "You will descend the thirty-three steps that are there and you will immediately walk straight ahead of you and without stopping for a second, until a hand seizes your shoulder and a voice says to you, 'Come, my brother!'"

The Temple door had closed again, and the heavy key had turned three times in the iron lock.

What would happen now?

No candidate knows the details of the rite of Hanging in advance, for what one can read on this subject in the various "testimonies" is limited to this:

"One descends thirty-three steps into the depths of the cellar situated beneath the Temple of Satanic Love, because thirty-three is the symbolic number of all those who, after the

Crucified of the First Night of a Triangle, attempt the experience of rebirth.

"The profane imagine that the hierarchical grades represent an ascension. Nothing could be more false! To know, it is necessary to descend.

In the narrow passageway, where one advances with difficulty, full of anxiety and not knowing the awaited destination, one relives in a few minutes all of the pleasures and all of the pains of his life. These memories present themselves to the spirit in a disordered crowd and one says good-bye to them, for certainly one believes that he must die.

"But a hand suddenly seizes your shoulder and a voice says to you, 'Come my brother!' You believe then that heaven is calling you, and a new heat stirs your blood."

The testimonies tell us further that the one to be tested is led by the hand that grips his shoulder into the interior of the lower room, where the seven Warriors and the twelve witnesses surround him right away and form a sort of living roof with their raised arms over his head.

Then, the floor begins to sink and the twenty men descend still lower, into the cellar called "of the executions."

There, the gallows stands, ready to strangle the one being tested.

The cellar is large, but one cannot make out the end of it, because a few torches provide the only light, fastened to the walls by long bronze arms, the metallic hands of which seem to curl their fingers around the flaming wood with a painful effort.

Nineteen chairs, whose high, sculpted backs look like phantoms in the shadows of the room, are arranged in front of the gibbet, at a distance of five or six steps.

The Healer-Mage places himself behind the gibbet, while the Warriors and the witnesses install themselves on their respective chairs, which they recognize by the label attached to the back of each one.

When each is in his place, but the Freedman is still asking himself what he will have to do, the Chief invites him to remove his hooded robe, saying the following:

"Brother Freedman, bold Hunter of the Brotherhood of the Golden Arrow, you who wish to die by ritual strangulation, in order to be reborn or to ruin your chances of it forever, shed the skin that blinds you and present yourself naked to our eyes, frank and sincere as you must be. Among us, no one criticizes a Brother, and whether you revive or you die, we know as you do that each one is in all of us. If you revive to the New Consciousness, your triumph will be ours, if you succumb, we shall follow you in the night. We are here as leaves of the same branch and here solidarity is not an empty word. Remove, therefore, your robe and be courageous and calm!"

At these words, with a rapid movement, the Freedman extricates himself from the violet silk that had covered him until that minute.

Frank and nude, he greets the assembly according to the

usage of the Brotherhood, extending his right arm forward, and directs himself to the gibbet.

The Healer-Mage places the rope around his neck and his ascension into empty space begins.

This is, undoubtedly, a tragic moment, and it is impossible to give an exact picture of it for the profane. Also, the testimonies that the Brotherhood keeps in its archives provide different memories concerning this point.

Some report strange things, bizarre visions that have nothing in common with what is happening on earth. Others tell about hearing astonishing music, still others speak of tears and heartrending moans.

But all of those who have obtained a very special enjoyment during initiatic strangulation, which comes from the precipitation from top to bottom in the body of the one hanged, of That which we call "Satan" and which is the Force contrary to the manifestation of God (= Life), declare that at the moment when nothing any longer calls the things of daily life to the mind of the one tested, he has the clear impression of suddenly finding himself face to face with what could very improperly be called the Infinite.

"It was," one reads in one of these testimonies, "as if an inexpressible beatitude had suddenly invaded me. It resembled a free and triumphant thought, not directed to anything and having neither subject nor object. It embraced all in its prodigious and unlimited burst, and it vaporized everything: the things of the past and the things of the future . . . Everything, in it, was without weight and without form, and there the stars did not weigh even a gram. And I myself was no longer anything within this immense joy, for I was everything and I erased everything at the same time. My joy itself was no longer a joy, and I felt it as a radiant emanation of my being, not even becoming light, because nothing stopped its rays, flying into the infinite . . . They tell me that this did not last more than a second, but I affirm that this second was of the nature of eternity. Besides, eternity is nothing other than an unreal point of duration, rendered real by its stopping. At that instant, in that only possible infinity, I seized the Name that no mortal knows. It is unsayable, because it is and isn't at the same time . . . those who say that God exists are as mistaken as those who claim the opposite, for if He could exist in his unreal purity, nothing of what is would be, and time would be no more; and if He ceased to be the moving point in what exists, everything would be dead and nothing would be living. That is why the most that one can say about him is that He is the One who lives, in the past, in the nonexistent present, and in the future . . . Today, having triumphed in the test of the initiatic strangulation, I know and I confess that God is living. I know that He is, that He was, and that He will be forever, because I have seen his unreal face, recreated by me during the Hanging. I was, at that sublime moment, the No in its total power, that is why I was able to raise up the face of my divine Adversary and give him his Name, as equal to equal. I was able to do it because, for a second, He was my creature and I his creator. The roles were reversed and, flying though space without limit, I was able to see Him set in the past. But, flying, I lost the life, His life, that is why I have come back to earth . . . What shall I tell you about his properties? Only this: He has none. And of his will? He has none at all. And of His plan? He hasn't any. And of His love? He wouldn't be able to have any. And of His foresight? Being caprice and dance and gaiety, He is what He is, He sees and does not foresee anything. He is all-powerful, obviously, since everything that is living wants to live, and He Himself is Life . . . But I also know now which is the true Master of this world, the Master of the organized, weighed, and measured Universe. Certainly He is the Son of the Other, for it is in Him that He is born eternally. He is inseparable from Him, but He struggles with Him, night and day. In this enclosure we call him Satan, and we are right, for He is the Adversary of God. His Son and His Adversary! The One cannot do anything without the Other, and their struggle is as sacred as it is eternal. While the Father has no definite will, the Son has one: to destroy. He also has a plan: to burst forth. He has a love: Nothingness. The Son is neither caprice nor dance nor gaiety, but He could *have* all of that. At the same time, if He got it, everything would die, for then He would have God in his power, and He would devour Him in devouring Himself . . . He could do it, but He will never do it, for none of us will serve Him beyond the test of strangulation and without us He can do nothing. We will serve Him in order to know Him; we will expose ourselves to initiatic death to identify ourselves with Him for a second; but having accompanied Him as far as the Door, through which one does not return if one goes through it, we will retain Him in the temple of our body, even if we should die from it, burned by too strong a fire. This is, with us, the Law of Life."

In another testimony, where the same statements are found, formulated a little differently, we also read:

"I asked myself if it was necessary to go all the way to the end, to dissolve the last point that still attached me to Life, to assure for Satan, with whom I had identified, complete liberation . . . Yes, this question passed through my spirit, but I did not have time to answer myself, because I was precipitated into a bottomless abyss, with a rapidity of which I have never known the equal. If up to that time I had called certain physical and mental privations and annoyances 'sorrows,' I now know that this word does not truly correspond to anything in profane life, for there is only one unhappiness that is real: that of knowing supreme felicity and voluntarily renouncing it. It is by design that I write the two apparently contradictory words one after the other, because during my precipitation into the abyss, it was certainly me who actively renounced eternal joy, conquered and rendered possible by my victory, and yet it is also very true that my will as a Free Man did not approve this

The Third Birth

renouncing, and suffered terribly from it . . . My Brothers, the Venerable Warriors of the Golden Arrow, will say: 'The Free Man in you was Satan, and He wanted eternal joy, but you, Freed Brother, you decided otherwise, because you were not only Satan, but also He who lives, being Life.' My Brothers are right, and today I say as they do, 'Satan would not be able to Vanquish God unless He were not His Son . . . The essence of the Father is continued in the Son, that is why the latter remains attached to the former, and He will never be able to completely disengage himself from the visible Universe, which He will combat eternally. For, who says God, says Life, and Life imagines and creates forms, always the same, endlessly new. Form is the prison of the spirit, but because the spirit is living, it will not escape it. The spirit comes from Life, that is its misfortune."

Another victor concludes thus:

"Here is my new rule: I will no longer pursue any unrealizable chimera, but I will encourage all those who still have this noble folly; and if it is given to me to live until the Dawn of the Third Term, I will do as the great Moses did: I will let the people enter into the Promised City, but I myself will not cross the threshold . . . Because now I know this: the useful artisan for human constructions is he who has only one eye open, the eye that sees only the visible. The other, he who sees the total Truth, having opened both eyes, cannot believe in utopias, without which human life would be stagnant. Now, stagnation engenders death, and does not liberate anyone. It is also necessary to apply oneself to limiting the number of initiates as much as possible, for fear that not all may revolt and come to enlarge our Army of Satan* . . . Glory to this formidable No[†] and to this unfathomable Sorrow![‡]

---

*[Naglowska is positing a bipartite divinity, analogous to the Dark and Light or Yin and Yang of Taoism. One part, for which her symbolic term is Satan, eternally opposes manifested physical existence, tending instead toward a purely spiritual transcendence. The other part, called God, is said by Naglowska to be Life, and represents the will to live, which is stronger than the will to die, which is why we are here. The "Army of Satan" therefore represents the group of all those who try to rise above "the red river of animal life," and so it should really be called an "Army of Transcendence." —*Trans.*]

†[This No represents sexual control and control of procreation. Were these principles to be widely adopted, there would likely be new dimensions of human experience, and many problems of the world would become amenable to solution. —*Trans.*]

‡[This is the sorrow, felt by revived candidates of the Hanging test, that results from having voluntarily given up the eternal joy of pure spiritual existence for a return to embodied physical life. In the No, which is "black" (opposes Life in favor of pure, unembodied nonphysical existence) and this Sorrow, which is "white" (having come from the will to live), we have a balance of the two parts of the Divinity, which is why Naglowska says "glory to" them both in the same breath. —*Trans.*]

THE NEUTRALIZATION
Of THE BLACK FIRE

The Healer Mage cuts the gibbet rope at the exact moment when the strangulation risks becoming fatal.

The candidate, passed out, slides down then, supported by the Mage, is carried to the bed of hay covered with a cloth of yellow silk, ready at the foot of the gibbet from the beginning of the session.

The Mage arranges the arms and legs of the Freedman, and gets his head into a comfortable position.

In a low voice, the Venerable Warriors and the witnesses say the prayer of the healing sleep, while the Mage takes up the incantation that will accentuate and prolong the unconscious state of the man tested, all of whose strength still belongs to Satan.

A quarter of an hour later the basement door opens, and the priestess-lover of the tested Hunter appears on the threshold, draped entirely in white veils and with her hair flowing down her back.

She salutes the Warriors and the witnesses, who give her the acknowledgment owed to her high mission, and approaches the Healer Mage, who gives her the necessary instructions.

Absolutely calm, she listens and inclines her head in sign of comprehension. She immediately stretches out beside the man tested, but in the opposite direction. She remains thus, immobile, for several minutes, then she raises herself with a serpentine movement, extricates herself from her veils, and presses her palms upon the knees of the sleeper. Like a perfect acrobat, she raises herself on her hands, as a living column, perpendicular to the body of the supine man.

Her face being turned toward the man's feet, her long blond hair falls over the thighs of the victor, communicating to them the solar vibrations with which it is charged. One knows, indeed, that a woman's head belongs to the sun, and all the more so to the extent that she has been able to preserve, as our priestesses of the Satanic Temple do, the lunar quality of her sex. The young priestess stays in this bold position only a few moments. Very slowly, and in four well-calculated movements—that of the legs, and then of the whole body lowered progressively to a low height over that of the sleeper, and the last two movements unfolding the legs and bringing the feet, one after the other, to rest upon the forehead of the Hunter—she forms a harmonious curve with her whole silhouette, and the Healer Mage immediately verifies the desired precision.

When everything is ready, the Mage pronounces the formula that favors and hastens the neutralization of the satanic fire in the man's virile member.

This lasts several minutes.*

The Mage verifies that the normal state has been reestablished in the body of the one tested, and he invites the woman to again take her first position beside the man, on the yellow cloth.

The priestess obeys.

Two witnesses rise then and bring near the bed a long cloak of black silk, which they spread out over the two bodies.

After that, the Warriors, the witnesses, and the Healer Mage exit in good order, leaving the couple alone, who must stay in the cellar of executions until the first light of dawn.

What happens during the night that follows in the somber cellar, at the foot of the gallows?

Here is what a twenty-six-year-old priestess says about it, who has become, thanks to their common victory, the bride of her Tested Knight.

"I had no doubt fallen asleep quickly after the departure of the witnesses and the Venerable Warriors, but I would not be able to say how long my dreamless sleep lasted.

"It was completely dark in the room, when I felt my Knight's amiable hand upon the skin of my belly. I grabbed his wrist and said to him, 'Are you behaving yourself?'

---

*[Naglowska's glossing over of this process deprives us of any detail about it. She has, however, hinted at it in more detail in chapter 8. —*Trans.*]

The Neutralization of the Black Fire

"'What voice is this that interrogates me?' he asked.

"'The voice of the woman who has watched and maintained the sacred fire of the lamp, still burning tonight for you.'

"'A woman, what is that?' he said.

"And he himself answered:

"'It is the Door by which we enter into the world and the Threshold, which we cannot cross to leave it. Woman, it is your fault if I am still here. Where do you want to take me now?'

"'I am waiting for the dawn,' I said.

"He sat up on our common bed and, pulling me gently by the arms, he made me sit up, too. We couldn't see each other, because the torches had burned down to the end. A fragrant lukewarmness enveloped us, and I felt it as a very tender caress. Several long minutes went by in a deep silence.

"He then pulled me to him and, as we were both naked, I felt the heat of his body on my cheeks and my breasts.

"He took my head in his hands and kissed me on the forehead.

"It was the first kiss that I had received from my Knight, for whom alone I had lived for seven years.

"I was profoundly moved by it, and he realized it, for he said to me:

"'Reclasp your golden buckles over your breasts, O adorable creature! It would be foolish to profane now what has been kept intact for such a long time. According to the Rule of this astonishing House, you are now my bride . . . now that I have known a wholly other felicity! Do you grasp the depth of this nostalgic exclamation? Are you ready to walk with me on a path whose eternal sorrow I now know and where nothing more will from now on be able to deceive me? Do you wish to belong to me in spite of that?'

"I said to him:

"'At the age of nineteen I was attracted to this House, whose lunar harmony charmed me. This was undoubtedly my vocation, because I still take pleasure in it. According to the Rule, I am now your wife; consequently I will follow you without asking you whether your path is good. What is important to me is you, because I love you, and it is not for nothing that they call me priestess. On the contrary, since, like me, your dreams now call you elsewhere, from now on nothing will be able to break the bond between us.'

"'Come, my wife!' he said to me then, and in the deep, mild night he knew me.

"At the first light of dawn, nine of my sisters knocked on the door of the cellar.

"We asked them to come in, but darkness still reigned in the room.

"The nine priestesses carried candles, flowers, fruits, and honey cakes.

"They draped me in white veils, while my husband threw the black cloak over his shoulders, which had served us as a blanket during this wedding night at the foot of the gibbet.

"We restored our strength, and the priestesses, my sisters, sang the morning canticles.

"In a liturgical procession, we left the somber cellar together, through a narrow stairway built into the thick foundation wall and which took us directly to the garden planted around the Temple.

"It was there, under the first rays of the rising sun, that we received the nuptial blessing, in the presence of all the brothers and all the sisters gathered together.

"Since that day I've worn, engraved on a golden medallion, the name of my Knight, and I sign . . ." (*Here follows the signature, which we cannot reveal because the Lady in question is still in this world and no one must know either her state in life or her true marriage.*)

The Rule of the Brotherhood of the Knights of the Golden Arrow contains, among others, this passage:

"The Freedman tested by the rite of Hanging can only be married usefully to a suitably educated woman, for knowing the inexpressible happiness of satanic* pleasure, he can no longer plunge himself into the flesh of a woman, and if he accomplishes the rite of the earth with his bride, he does it for his personal growth and not for his diminishing . . . We confer upon him, after the test, the title of Invincible Warrior, for such is then his quality."

---

*[Naglowska calls it thus because it is associated with the Will to Die as opposed to the Will to Live, the striving for spiritual union instead of physical manifestation. —*Trans.*]

TO CONCLUDE

We have said, since the beginning of this book, that it is written to bring to humanity's attention the merit of the Invisible Knights, who in spite of the night of time have been able to safeguard until today, and in all of its purity, the great Tradition without which men and women would be irremediably precipitated into the degradation of the lower animal kingdom, whence the return, if it is possible, is slow and painful.

But we do not wish to end these pages without openly proclaiming the deep veneration that we always have for the Holy Apostolic Roman Catholic Church, which for more than ten centuries has applied itself to usefully protecting the ignorance of the masses, for whom, indeed, the exact knowledge of what we have just revealed here could not be other than a violent poison.

That is why, having the obligation to obey other orders than those by which the representatives of the Catholic clergy are inspired, we hope that the latter will do what is necessary in order that the Truth contained in this book should not be heard except by those who are deserving.

We have written here some things that the Roman Church is bound to reject with horror, in order not to trouble innocent souls, but we know that, even as they are rejecting us, only the initiates of this Church will understand us completely.

Our other adversaries, the Hinduizers, the Theosophists, and Protestants of all nuances, do not interest us. Nourished by lies and by the remains of a past that has expired, they can do no more than devour each other among themselves. The jealousy and pride that has molded them will forever prevent them from reaching agreement and forming an army capable of offering serious resistance to the celestial lightning of the Truth. Having come from dust, their theories will fall back into dust, and at the last battle these "scholars" will not even be present.

But the Roman Church will survive the storm, and she will adapt to the new times. She will preside over the entry of humanity into the Third Era, and she will celebrate the Golden Masses, as is fitting.

It is to her wisdom that we entrust this book. May she do with it what she shall judge to be useful. As to us, it is enough for us to have done our duty in publishing it.

Appendix A
THE NEW RELIGION
EXCERPTS FROM *LA FLÈCHE*

The following is a collection of excerpts from an article that Naglowska published in the first number of her little street newspaper, La Flèche (The Arrow).[1] *It was the very first article in that first issue, which may give some idea of the importance it had in her mind. This article, published in late 1930, clearly shows that she already had the main ideas for her new religion, which she would develop more fully in* The Light of Sex *(1932) and* The Hanging Mystery *(1934). Naglowska signed this article as "La Flèche," a pseudonym she also used elsewhere, but it is unmistakably her writing.*

THE TRINITY AND THE TRIANGLE

The Breath of Life has a three-beat rhythm. That is why the Trinity is holy. First there is the Splendor, which tends in a downward direction, then the Profanation, which travels straight ahead on a level course, and lastly the Glory, which rises.

The doctrines of the Christian church have called these Three respectively the Father, the Son, and the Holy Spirit. They were right, for so it was in their time, but we say: the Father, the Son, and the Woman. We could also say, though for less delicate ears, the Descent, the Sorrow in the body, and the new Ascension.

The error of Christian doctrine has been to credit the whole Work to the Christ, that is to say only to the incarnation of the second term. Yet, this error is understandable, because the Woman (the Holy Spirit) can do nothing without the Son, and the glory cannot be attained without the previous profanation. The Glory of the Woman is the glory of the Son and in Her is accomplished the redemption of the latter. *When the left shall be as the right,* Jesus said.*²

Our epoch is that of the third term, because the divine Ascension is now beginning, and that is why it is only now that our dogmas can be clearly announced in the public square. Nothing is understandable to the crowds if the hour has not yet sounded. Therefore we give homage to the learned men of the

---

*[This saying is not in the New Testament. It comes from the apocryphal *Acts of Peter,* a work written, probably in Asia, before 200 CE. "Unless you make what is on the right hand as what is on the left and what is on the left hand as what is on the right and what is above as what is below and what is behind as what is before, you will not recognize the Kingdom." —*Trans.*]

Church for having been able to keep the secret until the end.

The complete text of our dogma of the Trinity is presented thus:

"We know that the Trinity is holy. We know that they are Father, Son, and Woman, that Their glory is one, and that Their life is eternal."

The reconstruction begins today, and the new means is brought by woman, or rather through woman. But we are only at the first light of the dawn. We are like a train of which only the locomotive has crossed the threshold of the tunnel. The cars are still in the shade, and no one sees the new countryside except the travelers in the very first compartments.

What they see in the new land is *the act of redemption*: the woman attracting the man no more for his degradation, but in order to reawaken in him the spiritual force that sleeps in a materialization of transitory solace.

This cannot be summarized—given the shadows that surround us—more clearly than thus: the man's companion, in the new land, offers the divine energy liberated in her not for procreation, but to bring about in her spouse the vision of the plan of the Splendor. How? One can only know this with long preparation, yet the train that we are in advances further and greater is the number of those who conceive of it naturally.

The hour approaches when everyone will know the secret, and it is then that the selection will be made. For there will be those who succeed and those who do not succeed. That will depend upon the inner purity that each one brings to the liberating test.

This will be the baptism of the new Religion of the Third Term. The respective merit of each one will be infallibly shown and the resulting hierarchy will be indisputable.

OPEN LETTER TO POPE PIUS XI FROM MARIA DE NAGLOWSKA

Naglowska published this "open letter" in No. 19 (March 15, 1934) of her street newspaper, La Flèche.[1] *It was the first article in that number of the paper, which perhaps indicates the importance that she attached to it. It should also be remembered that she dedicated* The Hanging Mystery *to Pope Pius XI. Some parts of this "letter" are amazingly relevant to the Church, and the world today.*

OPEN LETTER TO PIUS XI

The Pope of the Critical Hour

You have said, Sovereign Pontiff, that Christianity itself is threatened with death in this terrible time when nothing is still standing: neither faith, nor hope, nor even charity. The peoples detest one another, men tear each other apart, and women no longer know what chastity is.

Everyone wants only one thing: easy pleasure, fast, stunning. They look for that, because they no longer have anything in their soul, and their spirit is empty, because it finds nothing.

For a long time now humans have said to themselves, "Let's not trust in anything except ourselves, let's not believe in anything except visible matter and reason, which invented mathematics; let us chase Christ from our hearts and let's proclaim openly that God does not exist; in this way we'll be free, and we'll freely exploit nature, enriching ourselves."

A hundred and fifty years have sufficed for this materialism to bear fruit, and you are touched by it yourself, Sovereign Pontiff. Interiorly, mankind has become exterior, and the Church, of which you are the head, has followed in this movement. Night is in men, it is true, but it is also at the Vatican and even, alas, in your spirit.

Will you tell me that I am fooling myself when I say that nothing scares you as much as true faith in a woman whose spirit is not asleep? Isn't mysticism what you fear above all? You demand blind submission from your flock, because you don't believe that one can, in opening the inner eyes, see something in your Church, on your altars, in your doctrine.

Yes, Sovereign Pontiff, the crisis of the present hour is there: in the nothingness of your Church and the nullity of your faith. Nothing but ineffectual words come out of the Vatican at the present time, because they are not sincere. Even more than in the masses, Christ is dead in you.

This has been fatal, and you know it as well as I do. You are not unintelligent in the profane sense of the word, and you have understood, since the beginning of your reign, that Christianity can no longer be pulled out of the swamp in which it is stuck without a new Word, the Word of the Third Term of the Trinity, the profound truth of which you know as well as I do. You know that this Word was given to the world at the precise moment of your election by the Conclave, meeting in Rome, after the death of your predecessor.

You know, that if you announced it yourself to the nations listening to you, humanity would be spared many evils. Humanity, having touched the bottom of the abyss, is ready now to begin the ascension. But you prefer to keep it on the exterior precipice, because you are lacking faith in your own strength. You hope that, for better or worse, the world will stay as it is until the time of your own end.

This is criminal, Sovereign Pontiff, and it is quite doubtful that you will not be punished for it. The forces, still impalpable, of the new Renaissance are pressing in invisible crowds around your walls. The resistance that you show them exasperates them, and if it keeps on, the clash will be furious. After the unhappiness of the crowds, it is your unhappiness that they are preparing.

For you have two choices: either you will light the torch of the Third Term of the Trinity under your dome, recognizing that love is not forbidden, but that it must be made sublime, or the love that you chase away will turn against you, as a savage passion.

The chief of the Italians, Benito Mussolini, has declared that the new generations need a mystique. He proposes to them that of distant voyages and sporting wars.

Aren't you in a position to tell him that this is still only a derivative, an external consolation, when the sickness is inside of people?

This sickness is called the absence of love, and it consumes men, because women, no longer having religion, no longer know how to love.

All is false in our nocturnal epoch, whose only spiritual light is the vague memory of an expired ideal.

Have the courage to reveal the new truth, find the strength to say that man and woman are created for each other, and that in the love of the two is hidden all Mystery, all Wisdom, and all Mystique.

Allow us at last to understand Dante and Beatrice, without looking for noon at two o'clock.

I have dedicated to you, Sovereign Pontiff, my volume entitled *The Hanging Mystery.*

My wish is that you may deeply understand its form and contents.

MARIA DE NAGLOWSKA

Appendix c

THE NEW
COMMANDMENTS
AND THE
GOLDEN MASS

EXCERPTS FROM *LA FLÈCHE*

The following information is excerpted from La Flèche,
*No. 6 (March 15, 1931). This was part of what Naglowska
evidently intended as a formal announcement of her new
religion. She said, "We give them here . . . to launch into
the world in this month of March the first sounds of the
new music."[1] All of this information was to be part of a
promised future book, to be called* Les nouveaux rites ter-
naires (The New Ternary Rites). *This book, which was
unfortunately never published, would have contained the
details of the Golden Mass.*[*2]

---

*[It is probable that a preliminary version of the promised book accompanied
Naglowska to Zurich, where she went to live with her daughter, Marie Grob, at
the end of 1935. Her daughter thought that such items might have gone to Carl
Jung, but they have not yet been located. —*Trans.*]

THE COMMANDMENTS OF
THE THIRD TERM OF THE TRINITY

1. You will recognize God in yourself and around you and in the whole Universe, for all that is visible and invisible is the result of the Life of God, the only being that can say, "I am."

   The flesh says, "I was and I will be." Life says, "I am."

2. You will recognize yourself as the servant of Life, your God, or of God, your Life, and you will not adore any visible or invisible intermediate force, for whoever adores an intermediate force belongs to that intermediate force and perishes with it when its time has expired.

   Belong to Him who is, and not to him of whom one will say, "He was."

3. Do not give any name to your God (= Life), because a name is a prison and God has no walls.

   The name begins with the breath, and the breath passes and is repeated in another time, always the same, endlessly different.

   No name is eternal, how can you give one to Him who continues on?

4. You will build a temple to adore your God (= your Life), for your cares are impure, and you need a place to enter into, washed of your cares.

THE GOLDEN MASS

In the Temple of the Third Term the priests and priestesses of the Ascension will accomplish the act of deliverance.

One will choose seven men and three women* healthy in spirit, in heart, and in body, and one will ask them to accomplish the act of love for the regeneration of the human species.

This will be a solemn rite, preceded by chants and music and by discourses in conformity with the new truth, and one will drink the festal wine to show everyone that this rite is a joy that crowns long times of sadness.

The high priestess, annunciatrix of the new Term,[†] will signal the beginning and end of the rite to the assembly, and through her the divine energy, liberated through the

---

*[Naglowska's prescription of seven men and three women is found in many places, and she never deviated from it. It may be symbolic of the ten sephiroth, which in Lurianic Kabbalah fall into a group of three (Chokhmah, Binah, and Daat) and a group of seven (Chesed, Gevurah, Tiferet, Netzach, Hod, Yesod, and Malkuth). Another, and perhaps more tenable hypothesis is that she was influenced by the septaine (composed of men) and the trinité (composed of women) of Eugene Vitras. —Trans.]

†[This would have undoubtedly been Naglowska, had she lived long enough to "say the Golden Mass," as was her hope. It was not to be. —Trans.]

contact of flesh in the sanctuary, will be poured out upon the congregation.*4

The men and women making up the congregation will receive great moral and spiritual benefit from it, and their own vital energy will be fortified and sanctified thereby.

---

*[Probably in the form of a spermatophagic Communion. —*Trans.*]

Appendix D

MARIA'S
LAST WORDS TO US

HER PREDICTION OF
THE SECOND WORLD WAR

*From October 1930 to January 1935, twenty issues of
Naglowska's little newspaper,* La Flèche, *were produced.
By the time of the last issue there were signs that she
was slowing down, and she probably knew that she was
terminally ill. The last non-advertising pages of the last
issue of the newspaper contained two things. The first
was a peculiar, multi-voice poem by Naglowska, called
"L'Amour de la prêtresse" (The Love of the Priestess). I
don't intend to translate it here, because it is written
in a style that was already old-fashioned when it was
written and it isn't to today's taste at all. It's also highly
dependent on rhyme, which makes a good translation
problematic. One of the voices in the poem is that of the*

Priestess, with whom Naglowska would have identified. The last thing she says in the poem is "my soul smokes in a holocaust." This sounds quite foreboding. One has the feeling that the poem was never finished. Perhaps we'll have the answer someday, if Maria's missing works are ever discovered.

The other thing in these last pages of the last issue of her newspaper is a short piece entitled "Avant la guerre de 1936." It is clearly a prediction of the Second World War. If one considers that the Spanish Civil War, which was the preamble to World War II, began in July of 1936, even her timing was accurate. It is not surprising that she could not see past 1936, which was the year of her own death. Here, in translation, are her last words to us.

BEFORE THE WAR OF 1936

La Flèche has reappeared. For the movement of the Third Term of the Trinity this is an event of capital importance, and even more meaningful since 1935 is the last year before the great storm.

Indeed, for twelve more months men and women can choose their path and orient themselves, according to their will, on the side of the Light, or on the side of the Shadows.

In 1936, the two contrary currents, which must contribute

by their struggle to the formation of the ascensional line of our Triangle, will be made clear with such force that no one will any longer be able to act as he would like. We will all be carried away by the terrible winds, to the right, to the left, or upward, according to what we shall have done this year.

The war, in 1936, will be inevitable, because the hidden storm will have need of blood upon the earth.

The nations, which do not wish to founder in the coming catastrophe, can defend themselves starting now.

We wish and we hope the French people will be spared. We wish it and hope it not only because we believe in the large role that France must play, beginning in 1936, for the effective construction of the New Era, but also because it seems to us that the evil forces, notably those that are stubbornly trying to revive what is dead, have not found in France enough passive and devoted elements. Also, the historic Second Term of the Trinity, which is reaching its end, having really lit the torch of the heart in the whole French nation, has not been able to resist, under this sky, the lamentable decomposition of its formal foundations. A hundred and fifty years of will directed toward freedom of the intellect have not passed in vain.

But beyond the French borders the combat will be atrocious. Let us form our ranks, beginning today, to bring to the desolate world of tomorrow the vivifying Word of the Third Term.

NOTES

INTRODUCTION.
MARIA DE NAGLOWSKA,
"A RIDDLE WRAPPED IN A MYSTERY"

1. P. B. Randolph, *Magia Sexualis,* trans. Maria de Naglowska (Paris: Robert Télin, 1931).
2. Maria de Naglowska, *The Light of Sex* (Rochester, Vt.: Inner Traditions, 2011).
3. The "alternate" versions can be found, for example, in René Thimmy, *La Magie à Paris* (Paris: Les Éditions de France, 1934), 69–71. Also in Sarane Alexandrian, *Les Libérateurs de l'amour* (Paris: Éditions du Seuil), 186–7, which is more reliable. The most reliable version, though, is that in Marc Pluquet's *La Sophiale: Maria de Naglowska, sa vie–son oeuvre.* (Montpeyroux: Éditions Gouttelettes de Rosée, n.d.), 3–6.
4. Pluquet, *La Sophiale,* 3–6.
5. Maria de Naglowska, "Mon chef spirituel," *La Flèche Organe d'Action Magique* 10 (February 15, 1932), 2–3.
6. Julius Evola, *The Metaphysics of Sex* (New York: Inner Traditions International, 1983), 261.
7. Randolph, *Magia Sexualis.*
8. Pluquet, *La Sophiale,* 8,14.

9. Maria de Naglowska, *Le Rite Sacré de l'Amour Magique* (Supplément de *La Flèche Organe d'Action Magique,* Paris: 1932). A translation of this work is forthcoming in the present series.

10. Maria de Naglowska, *The Light of Sex.*

11. Pluquet, *La Sophiale,* 12.

12. Maria de Naglowska, "Avant la Guerre de 1936," *La Flèche Organe d'Action Magique* 20 (January 15, 1935): 3.

13. Pluquet, *La Sophiale,* 14.

14. Ibid., 7.

15. Alexandrian, *Les Libérateurs de l'amour,* 185–206.

16. Pluquet, *La Sophiale,* 14.

CHAPTER 2.
JESUS OF NAZARETH

1. Maria de Naglowska, "Satanisme Masculin, Satanisme Féminin," *La Flèche Organe d'Action Magique* 16 (March 15, 1933): 20–24.

CHAPTER 6.
THE MAGNIFICENT INVISIBLE KNIGHTS

1. Maria de Naglowska, *The Light of Sex* (Rochester, Vt.: Inner Traditions, 2011), chapter 26. "We forbid our disciples to imagine Satan (= the Spirit of Evil or the Spirit of Destruction) as living outside of ourselves, for such imagining is proper to idolaters, but we recognize that the name is true."

CHAPTER 9.
THE RITE OF HANGING

1. Naglowska, *The Light of Sex,* chapter 26. "We forbid our disciples

to imagine Satan (= the Spirit of Evil or the Spirit of Destruction) as living outside of ourselves, for such imagining is proper to idolaters, but we recognize that the name is true."

APPENDIX A.
THE NEW RELIGION: EXCERPTS FROM *LA FLÈCHE*

1. Maria de Naglowska, "La Trinité et le Triangle," *La Flèche Organe d'Action Magique* 1 (October 15, 1930): 1–2.
2. Willis Barnstone, ed., *The Other Bible* (San Francisco: Harper & Row, 1984), 443. "Unless you make what is on the right hand as what is on the left hand and what is on the left hand as what is on the right and what is above as what is below and what is behind as what is before, you will not recognize the Kingdom."

APPENDIX B.
OPEN LETTER TO POPE PIUS XI FROM
MARIA DE NAGLOWSKA

1. Maria de Naglowska, "Lettre ouverte à Pie XI, Le Pape de l'Heure critique," *La Flèche Organe d'Action Magique* 19 (March 15, 1934): 1.

APPENDIX C.
THE NEW COMMANDMENTS AND THE GOLDEN MASS:
EXCERPTS FROM *LA FLÈCHE*

1. Maria de Naglowska, *La Flèche Organe d'Action Magique* 6 (March 15, 1931): 1.
2. Pluquet, *La Sophiale,* 17.

3. Thimmy, *La Magie à Paris,* 72. "Je n'ai qu'un rêve, voyez-vous, dire la messe d'or . . ."
4. Ibid., 78. René Thimmy, calling Naglowska "Vera Petrouchka," said "Vera preciously stored up the effluvia of all these intermingled bodies."

BIBLIOGRAPHY

Alexandrian, Sarane. *Les libérateurs de l'amour.* Paris: Éditions du Seuil, 1977.

Anel-Kham, B. (pseudonym of Henri Meslin). *Théorie et pratique de la magie sexuelle.* Paris: Librairie Astra, 1938.

Barnstone, Willis, ed. *The Other Bible.* San Francisco: Harper & Row, 1984.

Deveney, John Patrick, and Franklin Rosemont. *Paschal Beverly Randolph: A Nineteenth-Century Black American Spiritualist.* Albany: SUNY Press, 1997.

Evola, Julius. *The Metaphysics of Sex.* New York: Inner Traditions International, 1983.

Geyraud, Pierre (pseudonym of l'Abbé Pierre Guyader). *Les petites églises de Paris.* Paris: Éditions Émile-Paul Frères, 1937.

Hakl, Hans Thomas. "Maria de Naglowska and the Confrérie de la Flèche d'Or." *Politica Hermetica* 20 (2006): 113–123.

Naglowska, Maria de. *La Lumière du sexe.* Paris: Éditions de la Flèche, 1932.

Naglowska, Maria de. *Le Mystère de la pendaison.* Paris: Éditions de la Flèche, 1934.

Naglowska, Maria de. *Le Rite sacré de l'amour magique: Aveu 26.1.* Paris: Supplément to *La Flèche Organe d'Action Magique,* 1932.

Naglowska, Maria de. *La Flèche Organe d'Action Magique* 1–20 (Oct. 15, 1930–Jan. 15, 1935).

Pluquet, Marc. *La Sophiale: Maria de Naglowska, sa vie—son oeuvre.* Montpeyroux: Éditions Gouttelettes de Rosée, n.d.

Randolph, Paschal Beverly. Compiled and translated by Maria de Naglowska. *Magia Sexualis.* Paris: Robert Télin. 1931.

Schreck, Nikolas and Zeena. *Demons of the Flesh.* Clerkenwell: Creation Books, 2002.

Thimmy, René. *La Magie à Paris.* Paris: Les Éditions de France, 1934.

INDEX

Page numbers in *italics* refer to illustrations.

BOOKS OF RELATED INTEREST

The Light of Sex
Initiation, Magic, and Sacrament
by Maria de Naglowska

Decoding the Enochian Secrets
God's Most Holy Book to Mankind as Received by Dr. John Dee from
Angelic Messengers
by John DeSalvo, Ph.D.

The Lost Art of Enochian Magic
Angels, Invocations, and the Secrets Revealed to Dr. John Dee
by John DeSalvo, Ph.D.

Introduction to Magic
Rituals and Practical Techniques for the Magus
by Julius Evola and the UR Group

The Complete Illustrated Kama Sutra
Edited by Lance Dane

Tantric Sex for Men
Making Love a Meditation
by Diana Richardson and Michael Richardson

Tantric Orgasm for Women
by Diana Richardson

The Complete Kama Sutra
The First Unabridged Modern Translation of the Classic Indian Text
by Alain Danilou

INNER TRADITIONS • BEAR & COMPANY
P.O. Box 388
Rochester, VT 05767
1-800-246-8648
www.InnerTraditions.com

Or contact your local bookseller